MEDIA

ISSUE 3 ▶

Guest editors
Anita Biressi and Heather Nunn

Barefoot
Publications

Editor
Jonathan Rutherford
email: j.rutherford@mdx.ac.uk

Editorial Office
Mediactive
Media, Communications and Cultural Studies Group
Middlesex University
White Hart Lane
London N17 8HR

Advertisements
Write for information to Mediactive
c/o Barefoot Publications
99a Wallis Road
London E9 5LN

Text setting: E-type
Cover Design: Fran Davies

Website www.barefootpublications.co.uk

Editorial Board

Contents

Editorial

Mediawar

Down went Radio 4 *Today* journalist Andrew Gilligan, followed by Gavyn Davies, Chairman of the BBC and then Greg Dyke, BBC Director General. The Hutton Report published in January 2004 left a trail of media casualties. Tony Blair's former Director of Communications Alistair Campbell announced at an impromptu post-publication news conference: 'What the report shows very clearly is the prime minister told the truth, the government told the truth, I told the truth. The BBC, from the chairman and the director general on down, did not'.

As we complete the editing of *Mediawar* there exists a growing feeling that history will judge Tony Blair's premiership on his ill-conceived decision to follow President Bush into Iraq. The impact of Blair's hubris on Britain's standing in the world has yet to be calculated, but back on the domestic front it has left a trail of damaged civic institutions. Not least the BBC, not least the concept of truth. In spite of the Hutton Report's conclusions, the evidence it presented showed clearly the Government's role in assembling the ambiguities of intelligence discourse into a simple argument for war. Yet the government was exonerated and the BBC lambasted.

As the war in Iraq continued to unfold into the disaster of the occupation, the *Daily Mirror* published a series of disturbing photographs showing soldiers of the First Battalion Queen's Lancashire Regiment humiliating Iraqi prisoners. The pictures were published against the background of the previous publication of images of maltreatment and inhumane abuse of prisoners at Abu Ghraib prison in Baghdad by US military personnel. The *Mirror*'s images were proven to be faked, however. Editor Piers Morgan claimed that they were essentially true. Out went Piers Morgan. In July 2004, John Morrison, former deputy chief of Defence Intelligence Staff (DIS) told BBC's *Panorama* programme that by asserting that Iraq posed a threat, 'the Prime Minister was going way beyond anything any professional analyst would have agreed.' – 'You could almost hear the collective raspberry going up around Whitehall'. Out went Morrison, dismissed from his post as chief investigator to the Intelligence and Security Committee (ISC). Yet, while senior media figures have been falling like ninepins, and demands for accountability have been reverberating through the corridors of Broadcasting House, not one Government Minister has resigned. Indeed, as the BBC faces the start of a highly charged debate about the future of its licence fee, vague threats have emerged from government circles questioning its autonomy and wondering aloud about the value of public service broadcasting.

The third issue of *Mediactive* examines the media's portrayal of the invasion and occupation of Iraq and the political and social consequences of reporting the war. During the debate about the veracity of the *Mirror*'s photographs, influential international journalists such as Robert Fisk and John Pilger cautioned that the argument had become a means to side-step wider debates about the role of the journalist, to weaken the power of the journalist's dissenting voice and put a brake on the necessary media dissection of the broader hegemonic discourses of war, security, retribution and 'rights'. This and other threats to the expression of critical voices in the media must be continually monitored. There is a great need for dissenting journalistic voices in America and Europe, on a whole range of issues that have arisen in the course of the 'war on terrorism'. In particular there is a need to focus on the diminution of civil rights that has taken place alongside the attempts to control media criticism. In the name of 'security' and prevention of 'terror', the law and ethical behaviour are being continually compromised. Giorgio Agamben has argued that today there are extreme and dangerous developments in the European and American political discourse of 'security'. When politics reduces itself to the role of 'police', the distinction between state-sanctioned violence and terrorism threatens to be eroded. A state that has security as its defining task and source of legitimacy 'can always be provoked by terrorism to become itself terroristic'.[1] In the new situation created by the end of the classical form of war between sovereign states, the search for global security can lead to a 'world civil war which makes all civil coexistence impossible'.[2] These developments raise significant questions about the future role of journalists and their ability to report war and crisis.

War by any other name

The concept of 'humanitarian war' has been prevalent in the last decade. It has littered the language of Western foreign policy and ranks in obscurantism alongside rhetoric that names soldiers 'peacekeepers', occupation of a sovereign state as 'liberation' and dead civilians as 'collateral damage'.[3] In this context conflict (rarely called 'war') is framed as an extension of diplomacy by other means, the promotion of diplomatic ends through coercion. The first Gulf conflict of 1991 (overtly designated a 'war') and the powerful role of the mainstream media in building consensus and in producing a media spectacle of a high-tech 'precision' military action has been amply discussed. Despite the fact that tens of thousands of people were killed it was perceived as a bloodless war, viewed by western audiences through the cross-hairs of weapons' sights framed by television screens. By the time of the Kosovo war commencing in March 1999, the British PM's press secretary Alastair Campbell went so far as to declare that 'the modern media has changed the demands of modern conflict'.[4] This implied that the media cart was being increasingly placed before the strategic horse in the decision-making processes that inform foreign policy, the practice of diplomacy and even military engagement.

The events of 11 September 2001 brought the vocabulary of war back into sharp relief and re-articulated it when the USA, in the wake of the bombing of the World Trade Towers, declared a 'war' on terror and on those states that harboured terrorists and promoted their agendas.[5] There was a sense, voiced almost immediately, that in the USA, at least, citizens already felt as though they were at war,[6] under siege, even if there was little sense of exactly who the enemy might be. The possibility of stateless enemies, of enemies motivated by incomprehensible drives, capable of crossing national boundaries and of using poisons, viruses and suicide bombings, inaugurated, in Slavoj Zizek's words, a 'new era of paranoiac warfare' and it seemed that 'war' was no longer a dirty word.[7]

Yet at the same time, people sought to educate and inform themselves of current affairs via the media to an unprecedented extent. Mainstream and alternative Internet news sites, 'blogs' and even newsprint sales soared. People actively chose to inform themselves about Islam in an unprecedented manner; books on Islam and Arab culture were reissued and sold in impressive numbers. Alternative sources of news achieved prominence and a sizeable proportion of the world's population became aware of the Arabic language satellite channel Al-Jazeera which provided, for example, exclusive footage from Taliban-held areas of Afghanistan. Even as official pressure and bellicose rhetoric swelled for the waging of war against terror and then against Hussein's regime in Iraq, so did a popular resistance to war. In Britain the majority of the press were sceptical of Bush's motives for attacking Iraq and commended caution and the pursuit of the second UN resolution 1441. The *Daily Mirror* came out strongly against the war and in the process differentiated itself in a crowded market from tabloids such as its main competitor the *Sun*. The *Mirror's* 'Stop the War' front page was pasted to many of the banners carried at the landmark anti-war march that descended on Hyde Park. It only paid the penalty for its radicalism when war began and readers shifted towards supporting the Government's military intervention and the papers that had promoted it.

The apparent groundswell of public opinion, as amplified by the media, that increasingly regarded war with Iraq as illegal, aggressive and rooted in questionable motivations of 'regime change', was counteracted in political and military discourse by a return to the rhetoric of humanitarian intervention. On the eve of war, a rallying speech by Lt Col Tim Collins to his troops was widely reported. Collins successfully wed bellicosity with a placatory vision of compassion towards the Iraqi people, which was in keeping with the tenor of New Labour's own rhetoric. He told his troops, 'the enemy should have no doubt that we are his Nemesis and that we are bringing about his rightful destruction … Saddam Hussein and his forces will be destroyed by this coalition for what they have done. Show them no pity'. He also added: 'We go to liberate not to conquer … Let's … leave Iraq a better place for us having been there' (*Metro* 20.3.03:3). This uncomfortable and precarious coupling of aggression and amelioration towards the Iraqis was central to the Government's media message and its battle for the hearts and minds of the electorate. It also suggests the promotion of another odd coupling – 'coercive diplomacy' – which fudges the point at which diplomacy ends and coercion begins.

It is arguable then that in political discourse, anxiety about the overt usage of the rhetoric and vocabulary of war is both present and obscured, and that this anxiety has become part of the organising framework of interactions with the media and with citizenry. What popular resistance to war demonstrated is that citizens living in what John Keane has called 'democratic zones of peace' do not perceive themselves as being apart from danger and conflict.[8] Rather they are concerned that they could be morally compromised by actions to which they do not subscribe ('not in my name'). Moreover, global communications and round the clock news coverage return distant acts of violence to the centre stage of 'peaceful' nations. Keane notes: 'The democratic zone of peace feels more violent because within its boundaries images and stories of violence move ever closer to citizens who otherwise live in peace'.[9]

This issue of *Mediactive* is about the present moment, representing work in progress on issues of representation, journalistic ethics, US imperialism, and other issues in relation to the war and its consequences. But it also seeks to pursue, from different perspectives, a broader set of related agendas that arise from the present crisis (but were inaugurated in previous crises) and persist beyond the end of the war. It examines the images and stories of war and diplomacy which, while they seem to address events on the geographical periphery of Western lives, are clearly symbolically central. It unpacks the ways in which political and journalistic anxiety about the usage of war rhetoric and imagery has become part of the organising framework of the media's address to its audiences. And it seeks to identify the future roles of 'media wars' – not simply in the literal sense of war as a mediated experience for the majority of citizens but also in the sense of the media at war with itself, a constant site of struggle over issues of interpretation, meaning and representation in the coverage of war, violence and atrocity.

Mediawars falls into three interrelated areas of interrogation. The first area concerns the discourse and values of democracy, citizenship and human rights and their articulation by political subjects and the media. Darren O'Byrne discusses the contemporary discourses of human rights and their appropriation by supporters and opponents of the war. He argues that the 1991 Gulf War can be defined as a neo-liberal war, whilst the recent war in Iraq marks a shift to a neo-conservative war. This shift can be partly identified by an agenda that slips from the neo-liberal protection of human rights as the desirable outcome of a campaign intended primarily to protect capital, to a neo-conservative protection of capitalist interests as a desirable outcome of a campaign intended to protect western values. Daya Thussu extends the debate about democracy by unpacking the revival and almost robust defence of imperialism as both discourse and practice within the context of the invasion and occupation of Iraq. He analyses this as a geo-political strategic form of governance and a core element of the unilateralist policy propounded by the neo-conservatives, whom he views as being increasingly responsible for shaping US foreign policy. The role of global communications technologies in sustaining this new imperialism is discussed to ascertain the mass media's function as a 'soft power' in the US achievement of imperialist aims. Ramaswami Harindranath deconstructs the elision of realist and non-realist tropes and generic formats present in the media coverage of this media spectacle to debate crucial connections between mainstream news and fictional Hollywood narratives, American foreign policy and the ideological potency of images of conflict that are sustained by modes of enjoyment structured in fantasy. Important questions about the relationship and access of the public to 'truth' arise from his notion of a skewed balance of relationships between the journalist, the politician and the citizen and the dissemination of information in allegedly democratic societies.

The second area of interrogation is concerned with complicating our reading of representations of women and children and their involvement with the war. Here notions of citizenship and its excluded or invisible subjects come to the fore. Furthermore, as Patricia Holland cogently argues, news representations of war are invariably shot through with gendered politics of representation. Whilst women have conventionally been excluded from dominant political representations of the soldier-hero they have nonetheless been central to discourses of nation, homeland and family. Furthermore, they have been present in iconic form as feminised emblems of liberty and as peace. Holland analyses alternative representations of three women who achieved iconic prominence in the media for their actions in warfare and political protest: Private Jessica Lynch, rescued from the Iraqis by American forces, Rachel Corrie, a peace protestor killed by an Israeli bulldozer in the Gaza strip, and Hiba Daraghmeh, a Palestinian woman who blew herself up in an Israeli shopping mall. She reveals how notions of femininity, ethnicity and nation weave through three disparate stories, which link the long standing Arab/Israeli conflict to the US-invasion of Iraq. The article provides an ideal context for thinking through the recent press fascination with the scandal of female soldier Lyndie England's involvement in the humiliation of Iraqi prisoners.

Máire Messenger Davies highlights the representation of children in war coverage and, in doing so, unpacks the generic role of children as emblems of pathos and suffering. She then contests this culturally dominant representation of the child by drawing upon audience analysis of primary school children and their responses to traumatic news coverage; illustrating their political sophistication and potential as active citizens. Here, she taps into current debates about the status of the child – as both representation and as agent – within a public sphere from which they have hitherto been largely excluded.[10] Cynthia Carter locates her analysis of children's online responses to news about war and conflict within the context of contemporary political and educational debates about the value of citizenship as a concept and as an educational resource. The insertion of citizenship as a core area of study in the National Curriculum foregrounds attempts to counter future voter apathy and disillusionment with political institutions by educating children in the value of themes such as community, individual rights and responsibilities. As with Messenger Davies, Carter highlights the few media spaces available for children to enable their active engagement with news media.

The third area of analysis is concerned with opening up debates about news production in a global, digitalised, market-led environment. The issues signalled here, whilst focused on the war and its aftermath in news production, extend key arguments about power, journalistic objectivity, ethics, control over material in a time-pressured volatile news environment and news professionals' capacity for critical self-reflexivity. Paul Rixon argues that the web expanded the public sphere in its provision of diverse sources of alternative information on the war, alternative discursive spaces and in its interactive facility. Through the spatial and temporal reach of the web, those with access were offered archival material alongside a diverse range of contemporary sources on the war. Rixon suggests that the volume and range of information carries potentially radical implications for different, less managed readings by global audiences, and for the way the information war is increasingly a key player in the winning of consent for military conflict. Des Freedman examines the *Daily Mirror*'s adoption of a highly politicised anti-government stance, in which its encouragement of active opposition to the war on the part of its readers confounded conventional disparagements of the tabloid paper as a depoliticised vehicle of gossip. He locates this stance within the media market economy, in which continuous re-branding of the *Mirror* has demonstrated the uncertainties of the political and economic environment in which the paper operates. Whilst the paper altered its stance as the war progressed, Freedman argues that the mobilisation of a temporary space of political dissent within a popular tabloid form cannot be underestimated.

The last two contributions to this collection engage with fundamental questions about the role and authority of the journalist as news producer in the accentuated pressure and restricted environment of war reportage. It is now commonplace in media analysis to present a radical critique of journalistic claims to objectivity. Such a critique frequently measures objectivity against analyses of how the news media produce and represent their stories according to sectional interests or the constraints of the production line. From this perspective, news bias is not in the eye of the individual journalist but is structured within the entire process of institutional news production. The last two contributions challenge the axiom that mainstream journalists' coverage of the war simply reproduced dominant messages without critically examining the hidden agendas and ideological biases of the state, military and multi-media conglomerates. Jake Lynch is Co-Director of the journalism think-tank *Reporting the World*, which was conceived as a discussion arena for journalists dealing with the ethics of covering conflicts. He has edited the *Reporting the World* seminar (15.7.03), in which senior journalists, editors and news professionals met to discuss the reporting of the war in Iraq. The result is a fascinating insight into the complex set of demands under which the news producer has to operate whilst trying to meet their professional obligations in the public sphere. The debate reveals the greater level of 'meta-discussion' undertaken by news producers than in previous wars and shows the value of asking media professionals to reflect on their work. They foreground the difficulty of filtering information when a propagandist 'dehumanisation and demonisation' of the 'Other' is a central aspect of war media management. Many of the contributions here signal the ethical and professional dilemmas under which they operated and their frustration with Foreign Office sources, and ambivalence over their possible exploitation as a government 'conduit'.

Finally, Ros Brunt tackles what she defines as an 'accusatory' mode of critique against media coverage of the war, which, she argues, ultimately lacks political and analytical efficacy. In contrast, she suggests an analysis that attends to the 'leaky' moments in broadcasting coverage, where shifts in political perspective or unscripted events signal a caesura in dominant news perspectives. Importantly, she highlights the need for a more considered return to the professional codes and practices in which the journalist operates and acknowledges, through specific examples of news coverage, and the way that 'balance' as a practice recognises concrete news events as inherently contradictory. Therefore, through modifications and qualifications of a news story as it is being produced, often live, news coverage has the potential to fissure hegemonic accounts of conflict. In conclusion she tracks the aftermath of the Hutton Enquiry in Britain and highlights the way in which editorial and journalistic impartiality has been opened up to public as well as media debate.

Anita Biressi and Heather Nunn

Notes

1. Giorgio Agamben (2001), 'On Security and Terror', trans. Soenke Zehle, *Frankfurter Allgemeine Zeitung*, 20 September, www.egs.edu/faculty/agamben.html (accessed 11.4.04, p1).
2. Ibid.
3. Philip Hammond and Edward S. Herman (2000), *The Media and the Kosovo Crisis*, London: Pluto, p1.
4. Philip Hammond (2000), 'Third Way War: New Labour, the British Media and Kosovo', in Hammond and Herman (Eds), *Degraded Capability: The Media and the Kosovo Crisis*, ibid, p123.
5. See Noam Chomsky (2001), *9-11*, New York: Seven Stories Press, pp15-16.
6. Ibid, p20.
7. Slavoj Zizek (2002), 'Reappropriations: The Lesson of Mullah Omar', in *Welcome to the Desert of the Real*, pp33-57.
8. John Keane (1996), *Reflections on Violence*, London: Verso.
9. Ibid, pp4-5.
10. See David Buckingham (2000), *After the Death of Childhood: Growing Up in the Age of Electronic Media*, Cambridge: Polity, Ch.9.

The discourse of human rights and the neo-conservative discourse of war

Darren J. O'Byrne

Supporters and opponents of the two Iraq wars have sought to appropriate the language of human rights to provide legitimacy for their position. This language has been put 'up for grabs' in the contemporary global economy of violence due to the increasing uncertainty surrounding power and authority. The language of human rights has become a free-floating source of potential legitimacy. However its meaning is far from clear and its use is far from consistent. This article argues for a discourse on human rights based on an alternative 'global lifeworld' which sees human rights as 'real social conditions'.

I

The recent military invasions of Afghanistan and Iraq have put human rights firmly back on the political agenda. Aside from the direct human rights implications of the wars themselves, related developments, such as the containment of suspected terrorists at Guantanamo Bay and the increase in surveillance, are typical of the extent to which 'civil liberties' have been eroded in the name of 'national security' since the events of 11 September 2001.

The discourse of human rights employed by commentators from different perspectives on these recent events is littered with inconsistencies and contradictions. George W. Bush invokes the spirit of human rights when he condemns the 'enemies of freedom'. Tony Blair similarly places himself firmly in the camp of human rights defenders when he announces that 'history will judge us'. Whatever reasons there may have been for both operations, few can or have denied that the Taliban regime in Afghanistan and the Saddam dictatorship in Iraq were responsible for gross violations of human rights. At the same time, many opponents of the military invasions have couched their condemnations in the language of human rights, arguing that the interventions are 'racist' and drawing attention to their 'human cost'. How are we to judge the morality of these wars (especially in so far as their illegality is in little doubt) when justification for them is seeped in such contested ethical claims?

The contradictions were less evident during the 1991 Gulf War. Human rights organisations had for some time been urgently lobbying governments to put pressure on Iraq in the light of the Saddam regime's brutal treatment of its Kurdish population. While this provided the war with an element of ethical justification, its legitimacy in respect of international law had also been provided by Iraq's invasion of the sovereign state of Kuwait. Many of us still protested against the war, of course, but the reasons seemed cloudier. Yes, military action should be avoided if at all possible, so, yes, a diplomatic solution that would protect the Kurds, liberate the Kuwaitis, and prevent unnecessary killing would have been preferable. But if such options had been exhausted, and given that in 1991 a permanent International Criminal Court was still a long way from being established and international law was regarded as a toothless tiger (some would say that little has changed in these respects), could we legitimately, ethically, oppose the war? For sure, anti-war protesters found some comfort in couching their protestations in anti-American rather than anti-war language *per se*. One of the more distasteful positions voiced from within the coalition, the position favoured by sections of the Revolutionary Communist Party, was to lend support to Saddam in his heroic David and Goliath-style battle against the imperialistic evil that is America! Such a position was uniformly rejected by the vast majority of the anti-war coalition – how could it not be? Protestors stressed that opposition to the war did not in any way mean support for Saddam, and it certainly did not mean the tacit acceptance, even forgiveness, of the regime's gross violations of the rights of Kurds and other citizens.

So what position did the coalition adopt? To a large extent, the 1991 anti-war movement prefigures the later anti-capitalist movements, opposing the timing of the war, its covert reasons, the influence of multi-national corporations, and the broader geo-politics of the Middle East. Here was a war for oil. The invasion of Kuwait prompted the west (and the United States in particular) to take drastic action to protect its oil interests, and because international law forbids the invasion of one country by another, the war was presented as a legitimate response to an international crime. The consequences of the military action for the Kurds, or the Kuwaitis for that matter, provided secondary but not primary reasons for war.

So, in 1991, an ardent human rights campaigner might have seen no direct reason to oppose the war, bearing in mind its potential benefits. Yes, the war itself was initially waged (and it is important to bear in mind that US military strategy changed dramatically during the course of the war) purely for the benefit of capital. It was a 'neo-liberal' war (I will explain what I mean by this shortly). But the fact remained that for moral as well as legal reasons, the 1991 Gulf War could be justified regardless of this fact. The contrast with the events of the last couple of years could not be more stark, and the ethical position is even more complex and contradictory, because the current military campaign is *not* (directly at least) a neo-liberal war, but a neo-conservative one.

II

Why is the current position so different? To summarise, in a neo-liberal war, the protection of human rights is a desirable outcome of a campaign intended primarily to protect capital. In a neo-conservative war, the protection of capitalist interests is a desirable outcome of a campaign intended to protect western values. It is wrong to assume that this apparent commitment among western leaders to human rights issues is merely a smokescreen for some ulterior motive. No doubt such motives do exist, but that fact alone does not diminish the importance of the human rights discourse. The current US-led campaign against 'rogue states' is an intensely ideological campaign, far removed from the *realpolitik* of those military operations driven by a desire to protect the 'national interest'. While the language of the military action appears to suggest a 'fusion' of *realpolitik* and morality,[1] the architects of this campaign are not 'realists' but 'neo-conservatives'; their motivation is not geopolitical but moralistic and ideological. For sure, it is perhaps not possible to fully disentangle 'realist' conflicts – pursued in the name of national protection – from neo-conservative ones designed to uphold western values or neo-liberal ones designed to open up new markets and protect the interests of capital. The interests in each case clearly overlap. They are, however, analytically distinct. It is not helpful for our understanding of these events to conflate them at the outset, even if we proceed to expose how the respective interests of the state, capital, and western culture are in reality intertwined. Certainly, the language of human rights takes on an altogether more meaningful dimension within a neo-conservative context than within a realist or neo-liberal one.

In itself, this is not new. Throughout history dominant powers have engaged in conflicts not to protect their borders but to protect what they perceive as being threats to their values. The language of rights has been as vital to conservative and neo-conservative foreign policy as it ever was to the 'idealist' liberals of an earlier generation, such as John A. Hobson or Woodrow Wilson. Historically, conservatives and liberals have both seen the international political arena as a normative space, an ideological battleground. US Cold War policy, and in particular the war in Vietnam, were largely driven by a desire to embark on a moral, ideological (for which, read anti-communist) crusade. The current neo-conservative position is disturbingly similar to the earlier one – 'western values' are under threat, and must be not only protected but imposed around the world. Perhaps the language of human rights is more explicit in the current political discourse, but nonetheless the message is the same. Among the harshest critics of the US Cold War policy were foreign policy advisors schooled in the classical realist tradition, such as Hans Morgenthau, George Kennan and Henry Kissinger, each of whom defended the classical principle that the task of the state in international relations is to protect the national interest, and certainly not to waste its time and resources embarking on an ideological crusade. In turn, Kissinger, of course, was heavily criticised from the political right for not pressurising the Soviet Union on its human rights record. Neo-conservatives clearly present an altogether different picture of the state of international politics. Who, then, are the neo-conservatives, and what are they saying?

Until quite recently, the term 'neo-conservative' was applied primarily to the contributions of various commentators on US domestic political issues. Taken together, these contributions represented a deceptively simple and largely cohesive perspective on the role of the state in modern society. According to the neo-conservatives, 'late capitalism' is undergoing a period of crisis. This crisis is caused primarily by an 'overload' of expectations heaped upon the state. The demands of diverse interest groups and consumers, the increasing reliance upon the state to act as welfare provider, and the influx of new 'post-material values', have undermined the authority of traditional values and institutions, and eroded both the incentive to contribute towards society and the Protestant work ethic which fuels capitalist productivity.[2] This overload of expectations resulting from the state's willingness to exceed its natural authority by pursuing welfare-oriented policies, together with the apparent primacy of the idea of 'rights' over 'obligations' and 'responsibilities', has created a 'culture of dependency' among a new 'underclass' of unemployable youths and lone mothers who have come to be reliant upon the state.[3]

The neo-conservative position is often treated synonymously with that of the neo-liberals; both are often discussed under the banner of the 'New Right' and indeed there are similarities. Both groups advocate reducing the role of the state in domestic matters, particularly in respect of social and economic issues (neo-conservatives have tended to support a much stronger state in matters of crime and policing), even if they arrive at that conclusion by quite different paths. The neo-liberals, however, tend to be free market economists and social individualists, disciples of Hayek, Friedman and Nozick. The neo-conservatives should also be distinguished from other right-wing interest groups, which are often included in the New Right label. Habermas, in an essay written in 1982, distinguishes between three groups who comprised the uneasy coalition that helped Reagan to power in the US in 1980.[4] Against the most traditional 'Catholic conservatives', the neo-conservatives are not necessarily committed to upholding the influence of religion upon politics (although there are religious undertones to their writings). Against the populist 'Protestant fundamentalists', the neo-conservatives argue that there is too much, and not too little, democracy in the United States.

The relationship between the neo-conservative approaches to the domestic role of the state, on the one hand, and foreign policy on the other, is tentative at best. Certainly, there is nothing inherent in the arguments outlined by the leading neo-conservative scholars (many of whom are disillusioned liberals or even radicals) that suggests advocacy of an aggressive foreign policy. Central to the neo-conservative 'overload' thesis is the need to balance the apparent over-emphasis on rights with a renewed commitment to responsibilities, so why should the language of rights be so important in international affairs? The connection resides, if anywhere, in the unapologetic moralism and culturalism of the neo-conservatives. Unquestionably normative and value-driven in their commentaries, they also view culture (meaning value-systems, in the Durkheimian sense) as the absolute bedrock of any society. It is this emphasis on capitalism *as a system of values* that distinguishes the neo-conservatives from the neo-liberals, for whom the capitalist project is primarily an economic one. Writing in 1982, Habermas was able to say that the influence of the neo-conservatives is 'more easily measured in terms of their intellectual stock than in terms of numbers of votes'.[5] Given the extent to which neo-conservative cabals such as the Project for a New American Century carry enormous influence over the current Bush administration, this is certainly no longer the case. It is organisations such as this that have steered the focus of the neo-conservative gaze away from national politics towards the international arena.

The point of departure for neo-conservative commentaries on foreign policy is Huntingdon's claim that the modern world is characterised not by conflicts between sovereign nation-states but between competing cultures and ideologies, or 'civilisations'.[6] Thus, the traditional focus on the 'national interest' is, according to the neo-conservatives, outmoded. Western values must be protected and extended in such an arena through the establishment of a 'benevolent hegemony'.[7] Among those values apparently under threat are human rights. Does this mean that human rights are merely part of a western discourse?

III

The 'freedoms' that Bush speaks of, the enemies of which he seems determined to hunt down, do of course constitute a very particular collection of rights, and this is where the neo-conservative and neo-liberal agendas certainly do overlap. The crusading defence of rights as possessed by individuals equates of course to a marketing campaign promoting the virtues of individualism as a social philosophy, without which capitalism cannot flourish. Such a philosophy duly reproduces the western Judaeo-Christian paradigm that perceives the world as the aggregate of the experiences of rational, possessive individuals. When the Universal Declaration of Human Rights was signed in 1948, the majority of its

Articles referred to such bourgeois, individualist, civil and political rights, firmly in the western tradition. At the insistence of various non-western voices, a variety of economic, social and cultural rights were added to the document. In 1966, the two Covenants, which translated the non-binding principles of the 1948 Declaration into international law, dealt, respectively, with economic, social and cultural rights, and civil and political rights. International law thus legitimated the split between these two groupings; a split that many commentators suggest was unnecessary and undesirable.

Traditionally, human rights are perceived as possessing three basic qualities: universality, incontrovertibility, and subjectivity.[8] Many 'postmodern' critics base their opposition to the idea of human rights on their rejection of universalism. They accept, largely, that the discourse of human rights is a western discourse and not applicable to other cultures and traditions. Some, such as Richard Rorty, want to convince us that, though this may be the case, it is no bad thing, and it should not require us to dispense with the pragmatically useful 'story' of human rights.[9] Others believe that, in so far as the language of human rights is inseparable from the language of bourgeois individualism, western hegemony, and orientalism, it is damaging and should be discarded. Such critics often invoke Foucault or Said to support their arguments, although both Foucault and Said were far too intelligent and subtle commentators to have made such reductionist claims themselves.

IV

Thus, the western powers have sought legitimation for their invasions in the ethical sphere – they were 'doing the right thing', protecting innocents from brutal dictators and torturers, championing (a particular understanding of) human rights. It is worth noting here that the western powers were happy to invoke the concept of human rights *as an ethical concept* with which to launch an assault on the political-legal structures. They have had no difficulty in separating political and legal institutions, such as the United Nations and international law, from ethical constructs, namely human rights. It is interesting how similar their stance is to neo-Marxists and cosmopolitan advocates of 'global civil society'. In their view, that the invasion of Iraq was illegal – and it surely was – does not and cannot automatically mean that it was wrong. Whether we agree with the war or not, we can at least agree with the principle behind this separation of politics from ethics.

Perhaps, then, those of us who marched in opposition to the illegal war have misjudged Bush and Blair. Perhaps 'history' will indeed 'judge them', and cast them in the roles of champions of right and good, rather than ideological imperialists. Perhaps Richard Rorty is right when he tells us not to abandon the story of human rights, because, even though it is only a story, and a distinctly western one at that, it remains the best story currently available. But the story is, of course, not that simple. How can we take Bush seriously as a champion of human rights when, on top of being the most trigger happy governor in respect of his eagerness to execute Texan prison inmates, he blatantly defies both the articles of international law *and* the spirit of human rights (remembering that the two are distinct) in his treatment of prisoners at Guantanamo Bay? How do we take Blair seriously when he shows flagrant disregard for civil liberties, democratic processes, and the separation of powers, never mind the rights of asylum seekers? With hindsight, of course, how can we ever have taken John Locke – the founder of the modern western bourgeois individualist tradition on civil and political rights – seriously, when he excluded women and slaves from his calculations?

Of course, neither Bush nor Blair will or should be remembered as great defenders of human rights, but they exist within a polemical discourse that allows them to act as if they are. It is because *western* society celebrates democracy, and promises the individual freedom from the tyrannical state, that they can invoke the invisible hand of human rights to legitimate their military actions. This is the problem with the political discourse on human rights – it is so dominated by western values as to close down any alternative definition of the situation. Human rights, according to the western discourse inherited from Locke, must be reducible to *individual freedoms*, freedom *from* state interference. To assume this is the only definition is to surrender to the simplistic world-view shared by those erstwhile enemies, the right-wing moralisers and the postmodern relativists. Why can we not find some consensus on the existence of human rights despite difference? After all, the idea of human rights is nothing more than a convenient way of promoting respect for human dignity, and the idea of human dignity is central to most (all?) of the world's major religions. Never mind that concepts akin to the modern understanding of human rights can be found in the writings of various non-western philosophers, even one of the great figures in western liberal thought, Immanuel Kant, provides for us a basis for human rights which locates it not in the purely political state-citizen relationship (the Lockean tradition), but in the ethical domain, in the way one should behave towards other people.

The west has always championed the Lockean tradition, and the individual freedoms (from the state) celebrated therein formed the western contribution to the Universal Declaration of Human Rights, which provides the foundations of the contemporary discourse. It has, of course, remained silent on economic, social and cultural rights, because these do not *necessarily* reside in the state-citizen relationship. The two sets are not, though, contradictory, and one can go so far as to say that the distinction made between them is a false dichotomy. After all, economic, social and cultural rights emphasise the structural conditions that are surely necessary for the full enjoyment of all civil and political rights.

V

It is essential, I suggest, returning to the unlikely Bush-Blair contribution to critical theory, that human rights remain embedded in an ethical sphere which exists outside of political discourse. To adhere solely to a legal definition of rights is, as Michael Freeman has recently and correctly pointed out, to strip the concept of human rights of its most fundamental premise.[10] To adopt a position of legal positivism is to restrict rights to the realm of state institutions. If we accept that human rights exist only when the law says they exist, we concede that they are solely instruments of the state (for the law remains an institution of the state), and thus powerless. The whole point of rights, Freeman says, is that they provide a source of legitimation from which to criticise the behaviour of state institutions. Furthermore, the ethical sphere within which the discourse on rights must be housed must be distinct from both the purely legal-political and the abstract philosophical discourses, in so far as it should be a pragmatic realm, rooted in everyday experiences and practices.

If Freeman is right – if the primary function of the discourse on rights is to make possible a critique of the behaviour of any given state – then are we not accepting that human rights violations only occur within the sphere of the state? If we are, are we not then accepting that hunger, poverty, unemployment, and numerous other atrocities which are not directly 'crimes of the state', do not in fact constitute human rights violations?

The simplest response is to deny the distinction between 'civil and political rights' and 'economic, social and cultural rights'. To do this, we should, perhaps, broaden our definitions of the role of the state. If the state is simply the servant and occasional arbiter of its individual citizenry, then its role cannot logically extend to the provision of a decent standard of living. But this Lockean perspective is not the only theory of the role of the state. Even Hobbes, charges of authoritarianism notwithstanding, provides us with a less jaundiced view of the state than does Locke. For Hobbes, although the state becomes the source of legitimate authority at the expense of certain individual freedoms, it nevertheless remains a servant, in so far as it is constructed to protect its citizenry. Logically, those forces that threaten the citizenry include hunger and poverty. The socialist theory of the state is thus a natural extension of the Hobbesian one. Above all, the state has a responsibility to provide its citizens with life conditions within which the freedoms and rights celebrated in the bourgeois tradition can be fully realised. That the bourgeois liberal tradition refutes this is not grounded in an *a priori* individualism in the concept of rights, but in the ideology of the tradition itself, and is thus not at all contradictory to the pursuit of human rights. Rather, it is inseparable from such a pursuit.

VI

Beyond the apparent certainties of the Cold War, the 'post-realist', globalised world is an intensely contested space. Late capitalism is indeed undergoing a period of sustained crisis – in this the neo-conservatives are in agreement with neo-Marxist contributors to the debate.[11] Both accept that the legitimacy of the nation-state has been challenged. One of the major consequences of economic and cultural globalisation is that the nation-state is no longer able to fulfil its obligations towards its citizens – it can no longer guarantee their security (from military, environmental or economic threats), and it can no longer presume to serve as the sole source of cultural identity.[12] The 'new world disorder' manifests itself as a 'free-for-all' in which money, power and identity become consumable products in the global supermarket, and in which competing interest groups vie for sources of legitimation detached from their presumed foundational bases. The language of human rights is now 'up for grabs' in the contemporary global economy of violence due to the increasing uncertainty surrounding power and authority following the legitimation crisis of the state and the de-linking of state from market. In effect, the language of human rights has become a free-floating source of potential legitimacy during this uncertain phase in the global political order.

To my mind, it is quite appropriate to treat the contemporary global condition, as many neo-Marxists have, as a 'global system', characterised by the presence of a trans-national capitalist class, trans-national capitalist corporations, and trans-national corporate practices including flexible accumulation in an international division of labour.[13] As with the domestic crisis of legitimation, in the global system the role of the nation-state has been seriously undermined. Critics of this position point to the recent displays of American hegemony as evidence that the most powerful nation-states can still flex their muscles, and of course to some extent this is correct. However, the wars in Afghanistan and Iraq, which I have suggested were heavily ideological and neo-conservative, do not in fact contradict the post-realist global system position. Indeed, we could argue that they uphold it. After all, the ideological struggle is a product of this post-realist uncertainty. But the global condition cannot be reduced solely to the dynamics of this global system. Global uncertainty has also breathed new life into what we might call the 'global lifeworld', the antithesis of the global system, which is articulated through the activities of campaigning organisations and global citizens. Herein, the language of human rights is even more significant, not least because under globalised conditions it represents a possible counter-hegemonic strategy to the dominant ideology of consumerism.[14] The neo-conservative warlords are at liberty to appropriate this language, albeit selectively, to justify their ideological crusades, but the language itself resides in this ethical sphere, beyond the legal-political paradigm and the false dichotomy it has created. In the post-realist world of uncertainty and complexity, activists and critical thinkers should not reject the discourse of human rights because of some presumed western bias, but embrace it in its indivisible glory as the basis for an emerging global civil society.

Notes

1. Barbara Hudson, 'Beyond September 11th: Certainties and Doubts', Phil Scraton (Ed.), *Beyond September 11: An Anthology of Dissent*, Pluto Press, London, 2002.
2. Daniel Moynihan, *The Negro Family*, Department of Labor, Washington, D.C., 1965; Michel Croozier, Samuel Huntingdon and S. Watanuki, *The Crisis of Democracy*, New York University Press, New York, 1975; Daniel Bell, *The Cultural Contradictions of Capitalism*, Basic Books, New York, 1976; Irving Kristol, *Two Cheers for Capitalism*, Basic Books, New York, 1978; Charles Murray, *Losing Ground*, Basic Books, New York, 1984; Murray, *The Emerging British Underclass*, Institute of Economic Affairs, London, 1990; Lawrence Mead, *From Welfare to Work*, Institute of Economic Affairs, London, 1997.
3. Murray, *Losing Ground*, op cit; Lawrence Mead, *Beyond Entitlement*, Free Press, New York, 1986.
4. Jürgen Habermas, *The New Conservatism*, Polity Press, Cambridge, 1989, p22.
5. Ibid.
6. Samuel Huntingdon, *The Clash of Civilizations and the Remaking of World Order*, Simon and Schuster, New York, 1996.
7. William Kristol and Robert Kagan, 'Toward a Neo-Reaganite Foreign Policy', *Foreign Affairs*, July / August.
8. Darren J. O'Byrne, *Human Rights: An Introduction*, Longman, London, 2002.
9. Richard Rorty, 'Human Rights, Rationality and Sentimentality', Stephen Shute and Susan Hurley (Eds), *On Human Rights: The Oxford Amnesty Lectures 1992*, Basic Books, New York, 1993.
10. Michael Freeman, *Human Rights: An Interdisciplinary Approach*, Polity Press, Cambridge, 2002.
11. James O'Connor, *The Fiscal Crisis of the State*, St Martin's Press, New York, 1973; Jürgen Habermas, *Legitimation Crisis*, Polity Press, Cambridge, 1976; Claus Offe, *The Contradictions of the Welfare State*, Hutchinson University Library, London, 1984.
12. Darren J. O'Byrne, *The Dimensions of Global Citizenship: Political Identity Beyond the Nation-State*, Frank Cass, London, 2003.
13. Leslie Sklair, *Globalisation: Capitalism and Its Alternatives*, Oxford University Press, Oxford, 2002; David Harvey, *The Condition of Postmodernity*, Blackwell, Oxford, 1989.
14. Sklair, op cit.

Mediating American imperialism

Daya Thussu

This article aims to explore the relationship between media and imperialism. Taking a historical perspective, it examines international television coverage of the invasion and occupation of Iraq in the context of the emergence of the US's new 'informal' empire. With the power of US-dominated Western television news, the Pentagon version of reality in Iraq has been projected to a global audience. The article will analyse the implications of this for the legitimisation of a twenty-first century version of a nineteenth-century idea.

Imperialism is back as a defining concept in international relations after the invasion and occupation of Iraq – the country with the second largest known reserves of oil on the planet – by the United States, the world's only hyper-power. The invasion, the most blatant violation of international law and state sovereignty in recent history, has interesting parallels with imperial conquests of the nineteenth and the early part of the twentieth century. Now, as then, the 'primitive natives' are being taught a lesson for being disloyal to His Majesty; now as then, the invasion has been dictated by geo-political and economic considerations; now, as then, the invading hordes continue to hold the moral high ground. No other country in the world could get away with the kind of excesses committed in the name of promoting peace, freedom and democracy than the US, and that too in the international public gaze, through its control of global 24/7 news networks.

Though the idea of imperialism and empire did not really leave the critical vocabulary, what is new is the discreet revival and almost robust defence of the idea. Even before the 11 September 2001 attacks on New York and Washington, imperialism was coming back onto the political agenda. Tony Blair's foreign policy advisor, Robert Cooper, had already called for a 'new imperialism' that allowed post-modern Western nations to impose order and stability on the pre-modern parts of the globe. Arguing for the 'need for colonisation', Cooper recommended active intervention to bring backward nations into the twenty-first century. Niall Ferguson, former Professor of Political and Financial History at Oxford University and now a star academic at New York University, has argued that the British Empire was essentially a benign and liberal enterprise, benefiting rather than harming the colonised peoples of Asia and Africa. Ferguson now sees an informal US empire in the form of globalisation (Ferguson, 2002). Michael Ignatieff, in what he terms 'Empire Lite', examines whether empire can serve both moral and strategic purposes. In this soft-touch variety of Western imperialism, Ignatieff sees humanitarian interventions as creating order in conflict zones essential to the security of great powers. It is imperial because the instruments of force are used in an imperial fashion – it is an American enterprise supported by other major power blocs – the EU and Japan (Ignatieff, 2002).

American imperialism in context

In the twenty-first-century version of imperialism, one can detect parallels with the 'informal empires' of the nineteenth century, when economic control and military coercion masked overt foreign rule; though with the colonial occupation of Iraq the US has even given up that pretence. As Andrew Bacevich has argued, the US mission is to create a seamless global market kept in place through overwhelming and permanent global military supremacy (Bacevich, 2002). Bacevich demonstrates that successive US administrations, since around the time of the Spanish-American war, have pursued a grand strategy of reshaping the world in its image, through free trade, military dominance, and, most recently, globalisation. Seeing Washington as the new Rome, he counsels that to maintain, consolidate and even expand this empire, the US should depend less on coercion than on persuasion.

The political face of US imperialism

In the era of globalisation, the notion of 'global governance' has gained much currency, though who is governing whom under the new dispensation is rarely discussed. The supposedly all powerful United Nations Security Council still does not have any veto-wielding representation from Latin America, Africa or the Arab world, nearly sixty years after its inception. With occasional disagreements from Russia and China and sparingly by France, as during the 2003 Iraq debate, the US seems to set or manipulate the agenda and when it does not suit its political interests, to totally undermine the UN system – as it has repeatedly done, most unashamedly during the Iraqi conflict. It is worth remembering that until 1972, Taiwan was a veto-wielding Security Council member, while China, representing one fourth of all humanity, was excluded from the UN.

In the post-Cold War world, the notion of state sovereignty, particularly with regard to those of the so-called Third World nations, is hardly tenable. Increasingly powerful Western-sponsored international legal and human rights regimes are being set in place to implement 'global governance' and it is being boldly argued that the 'international community' (the US) has the right to 'regime-change' in failed or 'rogue' states. An army of so-called non-governmental organisations is operational around the globe to legitimise the discourse of market democracy.

In this, the new American imperialism meets the old European one, with little imperial powers either echoing His Master's voice, like Britain, or negotiating to safeguard their own interests, like France and Russia. In the new imperial governance, Bosnia, Kosovo and East Timor have already become the first enclaves, followed by Afghanistan where new and old imperialists co-operated to make a protectorate of an 'ungovernable' country, using the United Nations. Iraq was an altogether different case, where new and old imperialists could not agree over who will benefit most from exploiting the oil-rich colony, in the absence of a UN umbrella. In July 2003, the empire's regional satrap, Australia, sent in a force led by its soldiers to the Solomon Islands, arguing that domestic chaos provided breeding ground for terrorism, thus couching the intervention in the language of security rather than humanitarianism.

The unilateralist ideology propounded by the so-called neo-conservatives (neo-cons) is increasingly shaping US foreign policy. Former Central Intelligence Agency director James Woolsey, member of the Project for the New American Century, described the invasion of Iraq as the onset of the 'Fourth World War' (the third being the Cold War). Under this dispensation, the nineteenth century idea of the Monroe doctrine has been globalised in the twenty-first century, making the entire world part of the American empire. In this 'distinctly American internationalism' pre-emptive attacks against those who oppose the new form of imperialism are proposed, with the invasion of Iraq being the first example of this policy. Having crushed its Cold War enemy, communism, the empire has created a new adversary, promoting a new 'ism' – terrorism. This elusive enemy apparently has transnational roots and therefore to slay this monster, the imperial hordes should have free hand to go for military action anywhere in the world, notwithstanding the old fashioned notions of state sovereignty or international law.

The economics of new imperialism

One key aspect of this 'Lite' imperialism is the way in which the US has managed to shape the economies of an increasing number of countries to fit into the neo-liberal, free market system. Multilateral institutions such as the World Bank and the International Monetary Fund (IMF) have played an extremely important role in this enterprise through the 1980s in forcing the countries of the developing world to comply with the policies of the Reagan/Thatcher era, promoting the privatisation of state enterprises. Under the Structural Adjustment Programmes dictated by the IMF and the World Bank, the economies of most countries of the global South were literally restructured to make them an easy target for transnational, free-flowing capitalism. The US – the largest possessor of votes within the World Bank and the IMF (17 per cent) – played a crucial role in shaping the global economic agenda, supported by its Western and other allies.

The creation of the World Trade Organisation in 1995, with its clearly defined policies for liberalisation and privatisation, further strengthened the position of free marketeers. One outcome of these structural changes is that the developing countries have seen their economic sovereignty further eroded, to the extent that they have very limited control of their own economic policies, now largely determined by the World Bank/ IMF/WTO triumvirate.

The combination of new communication technologies and the WTO agreements to deregulate key sectors – telecommunications services; information technology products and financial services – have accelerated the expansion of the US as the main economic power by creating the conditions for the emerging global electronic economy, creating the conditions to enable transnational corporations to trade on-line across borders, unhindered by national regulations.

Although the liberalisation of global trade has benefited a few bigger developing countries, notably China and India, for the vast majority of nations in the global South, new liberal economic polices have brought misery, as argued by Joseph Stiglitz, a former chief economist at the World Bank and a Nobel Prize winner (Stiglitz, 2002). The 2003 *Human Development Report* of the United Nations Development Programme, which assessed the impact of the 'globalisation decade' on economies worldwide, notes that in the past ten years, more than fifty-four countries have, in fact, witnessed a decline in their per capita income. It is instructive to note that many of these fifty-four countries are not from the global South: countries in Eastern Europe and the former Soviet Union – the so-called transition economies – have also seen their standard of living go down (UNDP, 2003).

However, what Bill Gates describes as 'frictionless capitalism' has brought unprecedented prosperity for the empire as capital can operate internationally in a deregulated, privatised and increasingly globalised bazaar. The transnational corporations, the biggest beneficiaries of globalisation and indeed the prime movers of a free market, have seen their power increase many fold. In this new imperial age, the TNCs have exploited the pro-market environment, notwithstanding the fashionable talk about corporate social responsibility. It is not surprising that the TNCs have incomes and assets bigger than the GDPs of several countries in Africa. In the freewheeling global marketplace, capital can move into, as well as out of a country at the click of a mouse. The electronic economy that defines so-called 'digital capitalism' can, through remote-control, ruin a country's economy, as seen during the 1997 currency crisis in East and South-East Asia, and more recently, and poignantly, in Argentina.

The primacy of energy resources to oil the imperial machinery cannot be overemphasised. Even before the invasion took place, the Pentagon had given Kellogg Brown Root (a subsidiary of Haliburton of which Dick Cheney was CEO until 2001) control of Iraq's oil fields under a no-bid contract. It has been argued that the invasion of Iraq was, at least partly, dictated by the need to protect the dominance of the dollar by ensuring that oil-exporting nations do not start denominating their trade in euros, as Baathist Iraq had dared to do. Now that Iraq is firmly within the dollar zone, the 'dollarisation' of other oil rich economies can move apace. In central Asia, the US has already expanded its energy interests – at stake are the rich oil and gas resources in the Caspian Sea basin, which may hold 100 billion barrels of oil. US companies along with British oil and gas interests control twenty-seven per cent of the Caspian's oil reserves and forty per cent of its gas reserves. In 2002, the Baku-Ceyhan oil pipeline through Georgia and Turkey was launched to bring Caspian oil to Europe, bypassing Russia.

The security dimensions of US imperialism

Underpinning its economic control is the empire's military domination of the globe. The members of the 'Project for the New American Century', many of them key functionaries in the Bush Administration, have argued for an expanded US military force, because, 'we need to accept responsibility for America's unique role in preserving and extending an international order friendly to our security, our prosperity, and our principles'. In 2000, just before George Bush became the President, the PNAC published a report 'Rebuilding America's Defences: Strategy, Forces and Resources for the New Century', which called for the US 'to fight and decisively win multiple, simultaneous major theatre wars', to control the 'international commons' of space and cyberspace and to take on 'constabulary duties' around the world (www.newamericancentury.org).

In 2003, the US had a whole range of overseas military installations – including seventy air force bases, sixty-five army bases, four for the marines and thirteen for the Navy, spread across the globe – from Australia to Japan; from Kuwait to Kosovo and from Panama to Pakistan. Before 9/11, only twenty per cent of US active army personnel were posted overseas: in 2003 nearly half the active duty army was based abroad, most in the Middle East, with Iraq and its neighbouring states accounting for nearly 170,000 soldiers (Thompson and Duffy, 2003).

The real power in the military no longer lies with the chiefs of staff in the Pentagon but is wielded by the five regional commanders-in-chief (C-in-C), as *Washington Post* journalist Dana Priest has noted, calling them 'proconsuls to the empire'. The C-in-C in charge of the European command, also the Supreme Allied Commander of NATO, handles Europe, Russia, Africa and Israel. Central Command covers Central Asia and the Arab world, the Pacific Command runs from India to Hawaii, while the Southern Command covers Latin America. Finally, the Northern Command, created only in 2002, covers the American 'homeland' as well as Mexico and Canada (Priest, 2003).

US supremacy in the skies has become increasingly important in the post-Cold War world. Deployment of increasingly sophisticated and militarised space systems is set to give the US 'full-spectrum dominance' for the collection of intelligence, communication and transmission of information, and navigation and weapons delivery. A new 'space cadre' is being created with the purpose of establishing global vigilance and the ability to attack anywhere in the world, part of the pre-emptive strike policy of the US.

In addition, the Pentagon is planning a new generation of weapons, to defend imperial interests under a programme code-named Falcon (Force Application and Launch from the Continental US), including huge hypersonic drones and bombs dropped from space that will allow Washington to strike its adversaries at lightning speed from its own territory. This will, in the next two decades or so, free the imperial centre from dependence on regional satraps and allies. According to the Defense Advanced Research Projects Agency, the programme is aimed at fulfilling 'the government's vision of an ultimate prompt global reach capability (circa 2025 and beyond)'.

NATO has emerged as an important security umbrella, its rapid reaction units being airlifted anywhere on the globe to defend US interests. It is now operating in Kabul with a new mandate, 'increasingly involved in security and national building. You can't do one without the other', in the words of NATO's commander for Europe, General James Jones (quoted in Dempsey, 2003). Following on the footsteps of the US, in June 2003 the European Union too sent its rapid reaction force to war-torn Democratic Republic of Congo. By mounting *Operation Artemis*, crucially without the US-dominated NATO, the old imperialists too wanted to prove themselves as global players as peacekeepers, resolving humanitarian operations and regional crises.

Mediating American imperialism

Imperialism cannot sustain itself by military power alone. There is a need to create and then reinforce the imperial perspective; one based on the notions of technological and cultural superiority vis-à-vis the colonised peoples, who are portrayed as subjects whose best interests are served by colonial masters. The mass media, particularly television, given its reach and influence, are crucial in making imperialism appear almost as a benign necessity to maintain global peace and order.

In his recent book, *The Paradox of American Power*, Joseph Nye argues that the US should flex its 'soft power' rather than its military muscle to achieve its geo-political interests, and thus cause less resentment. The mass media form a very significant part of this 'soft power', which has been globalised as a result of developments in communications technologies, such as satellite and cable, and particularly the availability of digital broadcasting. Despite growing media flows from non-Western countries (notably Japan and India), the West led by the US continues to dominate the world's entertainment and information networks. The major global players in most sectors of international media – news agencies, international newspapers and magazines, radio and television channels and programmes, music, book publishing, advertising, on-line media and films, are mainly Western-based organisations (Boyd-Barrett, 1998; Tunstall and Machin, 1999; Thussu, 2000). In 1999 the West accounted for 95 per cent of the world export market of light entertainment programming; 91 per cent of TV dramas; 90 per cent of imported movies shown on television screens around the globe; 87 per cent of all films exported; 72 per cent of all children's programmes and 62 per cent of all factual programming. Even within the West, the American connection is well established, the US alone accounting for 85 per cent of light entertainment exports; 81 per cent of television movies; 72 per cent of drama; 63 per cent of feature films; 60 per cent of children's programmes and 37 per cent of factual television programming (Balnaves *et al*, 2001).

In the realm of television news, there continues to be a structural dependence of the world's broadcasters on news footage supplied mainly by just two television news agencies – Reuters Television (part of Reuters news agency) and Associated Press Television News (APTN – the international television arm of Associated Press). Apart from these, CNN and BBC World – the two key 24/7 news networks watched in newsrooms and diplomatic enclaves across the globe – have profoundly influenced global television journalism. This 'US/UK news duopoly', can thus 'bestride the news agendas and news flows of the world' (Tunstall and Machin, 1999, p88).

Given this background, imperial wars are projected on TV screens as little more than video games. CNN's coverage of the 1991 Gulf War, for the first time in history, brought military conflict into living rooms across the globe. In the hi-tech, virtual presentation of war, cockpit videos of 'precision bombings' of Iraqi targets were supplied to television networks by the Pentagon, thus presenting a major conflict, responsible for huge destruction of life and property, as a painless Nintendo exercise. In this and subsequent US actions – in Somalia, Haiti, Bosnia, Kosovo, Afghanistan and Iraq – the humanitarian dimension of the military intervention was constantly promoted by the US media, often in a high moral tone. The responsible behaviour of Western forces in combat operations was underlined and the superiority of weaponry emphasised.

Since US-dominated television imagery is for consumption not only by US citizens but also by a global audience, this capacity to mould public opinion has a crucial international dimension. This dissemination helps to promote the imperial agenda to global audiences through 24/7 networks. Aware of the power of image diplomacy in the era of 24/7 news, the increasingly sophisticated propaganda machinery of the US government has successfully promoted a televised version of its imperial adventures to international publics. It can be argued that the world's view of US military interventions has been influenced by the US-supplied images: 'Operation Just Cause' in 1989 in Panama; 'Operation Provide Comfort' (in Northern Iraq, following the Gulf War in 1991); 'Operation Restore Hope' in Somalia in 1992; 'Operation Uphold Democracy' in Haiti in 1994; 'Operation Allied Force', NATO's bombing of Yugoslavia in 1999; the 2001 'Operation Enduring Freedom'; the war on terrorism in Afghanistan; and the 2003 'Operation Iraqi Freedom'; the invasion of Iraq. In these interventions, under the cloak of humanitarianism, Western governments, led by the US, have advanced their geo-strategic interests, whether it is in Kosovo (by changing the nature of NATO from a relic of the Cold War to a peace-enforcer whose remit now extends way beyond its traditional North Atlantic territory), or in Afghanistan (which has given the US government entry into energy-rich Central Asian region) or in Iraq (control of the world's second largest oil reserves).

The invasion of Iraq has been the most extreme manifestation of this imperial perspective. Blatant lies were bandied about in the media to justify the invasion: that Iraq was linked to the attack on 11 September 2001; that it possessed vast 'weapons of mass destruction' and was ready and willing to use them, thus threatening not just the region but the entire world. The media, especially television, has been able to represent an imperial invasion as a war of liberation, sometimes presented as an entertainment show, drawing on Hollywood. The rescue of Private Jessica Lynch, who became an icon of the Iraq conflict, provided an example of mixing of entertainment and information, with one news network actually calling her Jessica Ryan, no doubt influenced by the Hollywood film *Saving Private Ryan*.

Lynch, whose capture by the Iraqis and 'rescue' by US special forces became a major media story of the conflict, was in fact a morale-boosting staged event for the cameras. A BBC documentary later showed that the Iraqi doctors had actually looked after her well. One of the doctors who treated Jessica told the BBC: 'It was like a Hollywood film. They cried, "Go, go, go", with guns and blanks and the sound of explosions. They made a show – an action movie like Sylvester Stallone or Jackie Chan, with jumping and shouting, breaking down the doors' (BBC, 2003).

The toppling of the statue of Saddam Hussein in a square in Central Baghdad, next to the hotel where the world's media were staying, was another example of a staged event. Since the supposed liberation of Iraq the spiral of violence has continued. It is interesting to reflect that virtually every Western TV network hailed the killing of Hussein's two sons, Udai and Qusai and his fourteen-year-old grandson Mustapha – an act of deliberately killing civilians at a time when there was no war going on in Iraq. While Western troops killed in Iraq are given prominent coverage, the dead Iraqis – now covered under the broad blanket of terrorists – are not even a statistic.

There is a spate of recent writing eulogising the spirit of military adventurism. Max Boot of the *Wall Street Journal* insists that the US has never been an isolationist power; it has been involved in the internal affairs of other countries since at least 1805, when American marines landed on the shores of Tripoli. Boot argues that to maintain the Pax-Americana, the US needs to be a global sheriff: Americans have a historic duty to deliver nations from aggression, even to intervene in civil wars to promote 'freedom' and 'market democracy' (Boot, 2002).

This rhetoric has almost a missionary zeal to it under President George W. Bush, a born again Christian, whose ideology may be described as 'free-market Christian Zionism'. Bush announced the US victory in Iraq thus: 'wherever you go, you carry a message of hope – a message that is ancient and ever new. In the words of the prophet Isaiah, "To the captives 'come out' and to those in darkness, 'be free' ". In this ideological battle, the US soldiers are not mere combatants but missionaries, whose task is to bring salvation to the Iraqis.

While there is a sense that imperial rule is durable, history is replete with examples of the fall of empires. The Greeks were overtaken by the Romans; the Manchu imperial rule in China came to an end; Bahadur Shah Zafar, the last Mughal emperor of India, died in a lonely jail in Burma; the Austro-Hungarian and the Ottoman empires have vanished. Even the most dominant modern empire – the British – lasted just over a century, a short time in terms of human history; the Soviet empire did not even last that long. The 1,000-year Reich lasted a mere twelve.

The point is, things do change. Modern colonial empires were dismantled in the face of massive anti-colonial movements across Asia and Africa; after decades of apartheid, South Africa does have an African as its elected President. Many an empire has collapsed from internal contradictions and corruptions as well as challenges to its legitimacy. Will the American empire suffer the same fate? – if so it will not have a Gibbon to record its decline and fall. The 24/7 news networks will be there to relay it live around the world.

References

Bacevich, Andrew (2002), *American Empire: The Realities and Consequences of U.S. Diplomacy*, Harvard University Press.

Balnaves, Mark, James Donald and Stephanie Hemelryk Donald (2001), *The Global Media Atlas*, British Film Institute.

BBC (2003), 'War Spin', *Correspondent*, BBC 2, May 18.

Boot, Max (2002), *The Savage Wars of Peace: Small Wars and the Rise of American Power*, Basic Books.

Boyd-Barrett, Oliver (1998), 'Media Imperialism Reformulated', Daya K. Thussu (Ed.), *Electronic Empires – Global Media and Local Resistance*, Arnold, pp157-176.

Dempsey, Judy (2003), 'Afghanistan mission gives Nato new sense of purpose', *Financial Times*, 12 September, p18.

Ferguson, Niall (2002), *Empire: How Britain Made the Modern World*, Allen Lane.

Ignatieff, Michael (2003), *Empire Lite*, Vintage.

Nye, Joseph (2002), *The Paradox of American Power: Why the World's Only Superpower Can't Go It Alone,* Oxford University Press.

Priest, Dana (2003), *The Mission: Waging War and Keeping Peace with America's Military*, W. W. Norton.

Stiglitz, Joseph (2002), *Globalisation and its Discontents*, Penguin.

Thompson, Mark and Michael Duffy (2003), 'Is the army stretched too thin?', *Time*, 1 September, pp40-47.

Thussu, Daya (2000), *International Communication – Continuity and Change*, Arnold.

Tunstall, Jeremy and David Machin (1999), *The Anglo-American Media Connection*, Oxford University Press.

UNDP (2003), *Human Development Report 2003: Millennium Development Goals: A compact among nations to end human poverty*, United Nations Development Programme, Oxford University Press.

Battling over the 'truth'

Ramaswami Harindranath

Controversy surrounded the legitimacy of the US/UK-led invasion of Iraq and the apparent deception of Congress and Parliament. Crucial to this controversy are two debates which touch on the relationship between the media and society. First, the management of the narratives of war raises questions about the 'truth claims' of news and documentary programme making. Second, the accusations of 'spin' allude to the role of the media in the creation and maintenance of an informed citizenry. The reporting of the rescue of Jessica Lynch, and the marginalisation of dissenting and 'other' voices, suggests that partial coverage of events threatens the very values of citizenship and democracy.

In his introduction to an extraordinary book narrating the experiences of international aid workers,[1] the novelist John Le Carré claims that

> Instead of telling us what they see and hear, journalists in harness to the competing armies of the entertainment industry have become torturers' accomplices, mouthing phrases like 'collateral damage' when they mean civilians blown to bits, blotting out the screams and sweeping over the traces in their rush to present their nations' heroes in a pleasing light. In an era of supposedly unlimited communication, it is the truth-benders and manipulators, not the public, who are the winners. The truth is another country – the one that is inhabited by those brave enough to visit life's hells on foot instead of on the television screens.[2]

In that quote Le Carré captures a few of the main issues explored in this essay, those relating to news, truth, and conflict. Basing its main argument on the 'saving Jessica Lynch' story of the recent Gulf war, this essay will examine the textual aspects of news as a non-fiction television format, especially the paradox between its truth claims and its narrative logic; and attempt to take a critical look at the role of news programmes in the formation of an informed citizenship. What the Lynch story exemplifies, it will be argued, is the attack on the credibility of news, brought on by a distinctly and politically biased representation of an event whose textual characteristics share more with the Hollywood narrative than with 'objective' news. By merging the narrative of conventional news with that of mainstream Hollywood, the Lynch story, as it was initially depicted, borrowed from mainstream film the tropes of 'good' and 'evil', 'heroes' and 'villains', in a simplistic Manichean dichotomy. As it was originally reported, the story had less to do with reporting the event than with reproducing a distinctly Hollywood myth in which a helpless but heroic young woman is rescued by highly trained professional specialist American soldiers. We have all seen the films, and now the same story has been told as 'news'.

The making and unmaking of the Lynch myth

One bright spring morning in early April 2003, the community of Palestine, a small town in West Virginia, was mobilising itself to welcome home a hero. There was an air of the carnival and of celebration as men, women and children busily prepared the town for the returning wounded warrior. Yellow ribbons, the pre-eminently American symbol of welcome, redolent with military significance, evocative of a thousand acts of heroism, shone brightly against dark tree trunks and fluttered from poles. In a sense they formed a bright link between the town and the dreaded 9/11, the Gulf War, the two World Wars, all the way back to conflicts in which Americans had fought for 'freedom'. Television crew set up their cameras, lights and microphones, and journalists were everywhere, interviewing, photographing. The people of Palestine, West Virginia were proud to be interviewed – after all, it was part of the celebration. Their small, largely rural town had suddenly been placed on the global media map; all the news networks had sent journalists to the town; folk in Washington, including the President himself, had mentioned Palestine, West Virginia. Around the world Palestine, West Virginia would have a special meaning. The story, as it was initially told, symbolised valour, all-American bravery, loyalty to comrades. There was serious talk of a two-hour documentary, a made-for-TV film, a book, an MTV special, even a Hollywood film on Private Lynch. The incident had quickly become a media event, had been elevated to THE narrative that displayed a particularly Hollywood twist to the story. And all because of a nineteen-year-old aspiring school teacher, a young woman with blonde hair and a photogenic face, who had been 'rescued' from an Iraqi hospital following a typically 'daring' operation by the US Special Forces. That was the version that was reported when the *Washington Post* newspaper broke the story on 1 April 2003.

This particular version of events gained a wider audience through its depiction in other media reports. The *Evening Times Online* is typical: accompanied by a close-up photograph of a smiling Lynch in camouflage battle dress against the background of the American flag (the same photograph appeared on the cover of *Newsweek*), captioned 'NO SURRENDER: Pt Lynch did not want to be taken alive', the report stated that she had

> fought fiercely and shot several enemy soldiers after her unit was ambushed, it was reported yesterday. [She] fired her weapon until she ran out of bullets, an official said ... Pt Lynch continued firing at the Iraqis even after she sustained gunshot and knife wounds and watched several soldiers in her unit die around her, the official said. He added "She was fighting to the death. She did not want to be taken alive." ... The teenager was rescued by US Special Forces who slipped behind enemy lines to seize her from hospital in Nasiriyah yesterday.'[3]

As the language indicates, this account of Lynch's last stance became emblematic of the type of heroism embodied by Hollywood actors in the genre of war films – the 'never-say-die attitude' underlying many a cinematic mission into enemy territories. Lynch had gained iconic status as the young 'Miss Congeniality', heroic, intrepid, above all American, whose face launched a thousand t-shirts. One television reporter stated, 'This young woman has changed the face of the war.'

We shall return to the blurring of truth and fiction later in this essay, but it is worth noting here that a crucial component of this blurring of the veridical and the fictional in this instance was the supposedly 'live' coverage of Lynch's night-time 'rescue' by the special forces in Nasiriyah, captured on night-vision camera and edited into a five-minute film by the Pentagon for release to the networks. This footage was later included in the television news coverage of the event on networks watched by global audiences, rapidly making it part of the American folklore on the war. In a particularly stunning piece of action filming, the military cameraman captured a 'live' event that was largely staged for the viewers at home. As one of the doctors in the Nasiriyah hospital tellingly commented later, 'It was like a Hollywood film. They cried "Go, go, go", with guns and blanks and the sound of explosions. They made a show – an action movie like Sylvester Stallone or Jackie Chan, with jumping and shouting, breaking open doors' while the cameras were rolling.'[4]

A few days later, the *Post* ran a different version of the story in its inside pages which undermined many of the claims of the initial report, especially those relating to the heroics of Private Lynch prior to her 'capture' by the Iraqis, and her subsequent 'rescue' by the US Special Forces. The initial account was shown to be at best an exaggeration, at worst a complete fabrication. According to the amended version, she had suffered an accident involving the vehicle she had been travelling in, and had been cared for by Iraqi doctors in the Nasiriyah hospital. Far from launching a 'daring' raid the US soldiers could walk into an unguarded hospital and simply remove Lynch. The BBC's *Correspondent* programme, which included interviews with doctors working at that hospital, supported this revised version of events.

The ambiguous poetics of television non–fiction

One story, two accounts. But why does it matter? How significant is the relatively unimportant story of a young American soldier in Nasiriyah? It is significant, broadly, for two reasons: firstly, there is the importance of the time in which the event occurred, a period during the war with Iraq when the 'coalition' realised that the war might take longer than they had initially hoped; and secondly, it is indicative of the role of the media in formation of nationalistic discourses in times of conflict. In her documentary entitled *How to Tell Lies and Win Wars*, made soon after the 'first' Persian Gulf War, the journalist Maggie O'Kane claimed that the US government had hired a prominent PR company in order to 'educate' the citizens. The director of the company unrepentantly argued that the spurious allegations that had been made (with the help of a tearful daughter of the Kuwaiti ambassador to the US) about Iraqi soldiers wilfully destroying incubators in a Kuwaiti children's hospital was a necessary ploy to get the American public behind the war effort. That was a perfect instance of the media being used to 'sell' government policy. Truth was a casualty worth sacrificing in the interests of the higher good of a nation united behind the war effort. The Lynch story, while arguably not playing as prominent a role as the incubator story in the first Gulf war in mobilising the support of the US Congress, appealed to the American psyche through its use of the Hollywood argot, displaying in its narrative tropes from films such as *Black Hawk Down* and *Saving Private Ryan*, as well as other films depicting the rescue of American POWs missing in action in South East Asia. Significantly, it was reported that mainstream film-makers such as Jerry Bruckheimer were invited to advise the Pentagon on the packaging of news stories. As Kampfner argues in the article mentioned above, Lynch's 'rescue will go down as one of the most stunning pieces of news management ever conceived. It provides a remarkable insight into the real influence of Hollywood producers on the Pentagon's media managers, and has produced a template from which America hopes to present its future wars.' Even more than a simple case of truth and falsehood, what this demonstrates is the blurring of boundaries between fictional and non-fictional genres. The 'rescue' footage, deliberately echoing numerous action films in the war genre, allowed the transgression of the claims of non-fiction. The case of Jessica Lynch – including the event itself, the struggle over different versions of it, the attempts to manage its reporting, and its links with prominent Hollywood genres and narratives – thus admirably typifies several issues and debates regarding media and representation. The apparent 'liveness' of the footage, amplified by the impression of having been 'caught on the run', added to its alleged credibility, adding the 'bravery' of the camera crew to that of the soldiers. In her impassioned critique of the acceptance of documentary as speaking the truth, Minh-ha (1993) challenges the aesthetic of objectivity that props up documentary's *raison d'être* as a purveyor of real life situations and lived histories, and remonstrates that:

> Truth, even when 'caught on the run', does not yield itself either in names or in (filmic) frames; and meaning should be prevented from coming to closure at what is said and what is shown. Truth and meaning: the two are likely to be equated with one another. Yet, what is put forth as truth is often nothing more than *a* meaning' (p92; emphasis in the original).

At the simplest, Minh-ha is here questioning the truth-revealing claims of photographs or the documentary genre, of 'recording' events as they occur. From this perspective, the assertion that 'the camera never lies' is at best an exaggeration. What is often presented as objective truth is to Minh-ha a partial angle, or one point of view. In the Lynch story, as it was originally reported on television, the gap between truth and meaning is even wider. In terms of recording an event 'on the run', what it captured was an alleged rescue, whereas in the revised reports which appeared subsequently, the 'rescue' was unnecessary.

And yet, in purely textual terms, the 'liveness' conformed to the characteristics of the news genre, while simultaneously echoing the central theme of several Hollywood films. Two significant elements relating to the poetics and politics of representation need to be examined in this context: the narrative element in news and documentary genres; and cinema and ideology. The story of Jessica Lynch, as we shall see, problematises these two issues further, making explicit the ways in which the enduring virility of the Hollywood narrative and myth violates the truth-claims of the news and current affairs genres. By collapsing the textual differences between the two forms of representation, and through the active construction of the 'rescue' footage, the Lynch episode undermines the news genre's claim to objective truth. Narrative becomes the driving logic, with its beginning, middle and end, a climax and a denouement, and finally a happy closure in the form of her rescue. In presenting Lynch as an all-American heroine captured by the evil enemy, the narrative sets up a conflict which is subsequently resolved in the fashion of established generic conventions of war films. Crucially, the initial report on television news blended together the modalities of fiction and non-fiction, mingling thereby the referents of the elements of the report. In other words, in constructing the news report along the lines of a mainstream film narrative, the extra-textual references (that is, the relationship between what was being depicted and its relationship to the outside world) were mingled in particular ways.

Let us digress for a moment in order to assess the specific characteristics of non-fiction genres. The status of non-fiction television genres, such as documentary, current affairs, and news programmes, elevates them above narrative fiction in the hierarchy of truth in televisual representation. The truth-claims of these genres – in other words their fundamental difference with fiction in terms of their relationship with the world they represent – ride on a basic assumption that what they depict is the 'real'. Corner and Richardson's (1986) point about documentaries, that 'they have regularly sought to present audiences with accounts in which the viewed is to be taken as effectively indistinguishable from the real' (p141), also covers the news. The authority of non-fiction formats derives from this transparency: while certain expository devices make them recognisable as non-fiction, their credibility is dependent on their successful mimesis, that is, their ability to 'mirror' or mimic the external reality which they claim to represent. Conversely, the viewer, responding to the textual cues and conventions of news and documentaries which mark them as different from fictional genres such as soaps or feature films, willingly responds to the collapse of the distance between the sign and the referent that contributes to the literalism of non-fiction discourse. In accepting their claims to truth, the world of the documentary and the news is taken to be the 'real' world. With regard to our particular case study, the 'rescue' footage filmed with night-vision cameras, replicating the textual strategies of several night-time rescues in feature films, is presented as 'live' footage from a war zone, thereby assuming the status of non-fiction, a real event captured by a television news crew.

Theoretical discussions on the ambivalence of the documentary genre are, to a large extent, applicable to news programmes, particularly with regard to the differences between fiction and non-fiction. As Silverstone (1986) demonstrates, the mythic and the mimetic elements of documentary discourse interweave argument and story, reason and emotion, and contain the rhetoric of persuasion as well as expressions of the film-maker's reality. Such a conception of documentary incorporates the 'truth claims' as well as the ineluctable fictive elements in non-fiction. Wilson (1993) similarly argues for a case for documentary as primarily mimetic. His identification of drama as 'diegetic' and documentary as 'mimetic', a distinction with which he seeks to oppose narrative and non-narrative, is predicated on the assumption that:

> drama and documentary television assume different relationships between the text and the non-textual. Drama is first and foremost the production of diegetic space and time constructed around narrative. Documentary, however, foregrounds a space and time employed in mimesis, a copying of the pre-textual' (p118).

The selection of representational images in drama is therefore driven by narrative logic: 'in dramatic narratives the construction of the discursive precedes and determines the selective appropriation of the non-discursive' (p119). Drama is construction, and dramatic discourse creative, imaginary, full of artifice. Documentary, on the other hand, privileges the real: it is description and showing rather than narration, in which images are functional, not to the 'requirements of narrative', but to facilitate the viewer to get acquainted with historical reality: 'Here [in documentary] the non-discursive precedes and determines the discursive' (p120). Pre-textual reality is paramount, while the actual processes of exposition and narration are geared towards appropriating and conveying this reality.

The severity of Wilson's demarcation of dramaturgical and documentary spaces, while useful in highlighting some of the specific features of the genre, does not take into account the ambivalence of non-fiction discourse. The discourse of documentary straddles two domains: in its ontological claims it privileges the 'truth', while its aesthetic is strongly narrative in character. Documentaries are in this sense 'true stories', and their poetics resonate with the ambiguities contained in that oxymoron. Conceiving narrative as a cognitive schema, Gripsrud (2002) approaches this apparent paradox from a different direction:

> since the narrative is a way of thinking, a cognitive schema, it is also evident that it need not be fictional. The minimal definition of a narrative ... will therefore apply to many news items in papers, and on radio and television. News items are, in English, also often referred to precisely as *stories*. There are reasons to emphasise this: *narratives are not necessarily fictions*' (p194; emphasis in the original).

Fiction derives its logic from its internal consistencies of plot, narrative and character, whereas documentary's existence is dependent upon the accuracy of its representation of the historical world. The distinction to be made here is between credibility and authenticity: although the plot and narrative have to be credible, the issue of authenticity does not arise in the world of fiction, whereas in non-fiction there is an actual, historical world against which its images can be checked. The measure of the authenticity of documentaries and news programmes lies in their approximation to historical reality; and their credibility derives its force not just from the 'created world' of the text, but also, and more significantly, from their association with the world they represent. Despite its inevitable fictional elements, non-fiction stands apart from fictional representation through its avowed appropriation and reflection of the real world, and consequently, its social relevance. The Lynch story exemplifies the ways in which this relationship between the textual and the extra-textual can be exploited in order to present a particular ideological stance.

Hollywood narratives, ideology, and democracy

Armes (1974) presents a convincing argument on the role television played in revising cinema's appropriation of realism: 'One of the central preoccupations of twentieth century art', he claims, 'has been to redefine the boundaries of the actual and the illusory.' But while cinema contributed to this by successfully exploiting the link between photographic reproduction and 'reality', the advent of television changed the nature of realistic representation in the cinema: 'In particular, those directors who have sought to combine the naturalistic potential of the television form with the greater flexibility that film-making methods afford have modified our view of what a realist film is' (pp76-77). The first version of the Jessica Lynch story reversed this, since, as we saw earlier, the textual aspects of the footage clearly reproduced dominant Hollywood narratives and themes. But why does it matter? In order to explore that we will have to go beyond the merely textual and examine the ideological elements of the story.

In his analysis of war films produced in Hollywood, Kellner (1995) makes a crucial connection between mainstream narrative and American policy:

> the popularity of the film *Rambo* and the Stallone, Chuck Norris, and other 'action-adventure' vehicles suggests that the Hollywood President and large segments of the country had assimilated the Manichean worldview from Hollywood whereby 'the enemy' is so evil and 'we' are so good that only violence can eliminate threats to our well-being. Thus Reagan's most 'popular' acts were his invasion of Grenada and the bombing of Libya – precisely the sort of 'action' celebrated in *Rambo*, *Top Gun*, *Iron Eagle*, and the other militarist epics of the Reagan era (p74).

Even more tellingly: 'Hollywood films therefore provided iconography which helped mobilise support for conservative and militarist political agendas' (p74). His argument about Hollywood iconography is particularly significant to our discussion: if, as he notes, shots of helicopters landing in Grenada reproduced the excitement and emotional charge of Hollywood films, the consequent positive reception of 'real' news footage containing such iconography set the tone for the filming and presentation of the alleged rescue of Jessica Lynch. In the latter case, the complimentarity that we noted of the truth-claims of non-fiction television genres and the restatement of well-known Hollywood tropes is particularly resonant as it chimes closely with the prevalent post-9/11 political climate in the United States.

Analysing the discursive aspects of the television coverage of the 1991 Gulf War, Kellner argues that: 'the mainstream media became a conduit for the Bush Administration and Pentagon policies and rarely allowed criticism of its positions, disinformation, and atrocities during the war' (p210). The media, he claims, presented the war as an exciting adventure, 'a nightly miniseries with dramatic conflict, action and adventure, danger to allied troops and civilians, evil perpetuated by the evil Iraqis, and heroics performed by American military planners, technology, and troops' (p210). The parallels are so stark that he could have written these lines about the 2003 Gulf War. By echoing the dominant narrative techniques and forms of Hollywood, the original footage covering the 'rescue' of Private Lynch reproduced the ideology of dominant cinematic representations of war, ranging from Vietnam films to more recent films with Afghans and Muslims as villains. The Manichean dichotomy persists, whereby the 'good' Americans are victorious over the 'evil' Russian/German/Vietcong/Afghan/Iraqi. On the most overt level, this reflects the political rhetoric that reduces conflicts to those between the forces of 'good' and 'evil', which figured so prominently in various speeches by American leaders. If the *Rambo* series of films dovetailed American foreign policy at the time of the first President Bush, the more recent ones mirror and support the policies of the current US administration. The ideological role of popular forms of the moving image thus lends weight to stories of Hollywood producers being hired by the administration to help them with the management of the media.

In the case of the Lynch story, this is further compounded and complicated by the fact that this was not merely a feature film or drama which was revealed as an ideological vehicle. The staging of the 'rescue', which contributed to the footage, made use of visuals and imagery borrowed from feature films and television dramas depicting night time rescues of wounded soldiers and 'comrades' behind enemy lines. In doing so it neatly reversed Armes's argument about television's influence on film realism mentioned earlier: in this case television borrowed various features from feature film to augment a genre (news) usually associated with, and claiming, objectivity, neutrality, and 'truth'. In doing so it also presented the news (falsely, as it turned out) as an adventure narrative, thus extending the ideological character of numerous war films. News as information was as a result combined with television as entertainment, contributing to a powerful process of mythologising of the conflict. The ideological potency of this mixture becomes clear if we employ Zizek's (1989) format for the criticism of ideology: that it has two complementary procedures, '*discursive*, the "symptomal reading" of the ideological text'; and extracting the kernel of *enjoyment*, that is, 'articulating the way in which – beyond meaning but at the same time internal to it – an ideology implies, manipulates, produces a pre-ideological enjoyment structured in fantasy' (p125; emphasis in the original). While Zizek attempts to bring in Lacanian psychoanalysis to ideology critique, we can clearly see the usefulness of his complementary procedures in the Lynch case, particularly the link between ideology and enjoyment.

The unsettling, and increasingly overt, links between the state and the media threaten to undermine (some would claim has already undermined) the ideals of democratic society. If, from the 60s until the late 80s, the US administration used the threat of communism to its society as a way of controlling the media, as Herman (1995) argues, in the 21st century communism has been replaced by terrorism. Indeed, replacing 'communism' with 'terrorism' in Herman's argument brings it up to date as a commentary on contemporary media and society:

> The ongoing conflicts and well-publicized abuses of communist states contributed for decades to elevating opposition to communism to a first principle of U.S. ideology and politics. This ideology has helped mobilize the populace against an enemy, and because the concept of 'communism' is fuzzy, it can be used against anybody advocating policies threatening property interests or supportive of accommodation with communist states, or any kind of radicalism (p88).

The ability to engineer 'necessary illusions' in democratic societies as identified by Chomsky (1989) is concentrated in the hands of the social and political elite, an oligarchy whose power and presence undermines democratic ideals. Moreover, the collapsing of the fiction/non-fiction divide, and the consequent blurring of the modalities of representation, removes from news stories such as that of Lynch, and by extension the coverage of the war itself, their claim to truth, thereby threatening the unspoken contract between the media and the public, especially the role of the media as the primary vehicle for the dissemination of objective information. The balance of the relationship between the 'three key players in media-society relations … the journalist (media), the politician (government) and the citizen (people)' (Nordenstreng, 1995, p118) in a democracy becomes skewed.

It is important to note at this point that what has been presented here as an illustration of the abuse of state and media power should not be read as blind support for the 'other side'. Manipulation of media representations and policies is very much part of contemporary conflicts, in which every side is guilty of attempting to doctor 'reality'. The cliché is right: truth IS a casualty in war. As Hamelink (1995) notes, 'the forces behind the new world order and their fundamentalist opponents divide our planet in endless repetitions of "us" and "them" conflicts' (p35). What this requires is unceasing vigilance from us, the public, against being 'taken in' by either of the opposing accounts. Furthermore, as he argues, 'the most effective remedy is to achieve a level of distance from our own sectional interests that allows us to see [everyone's life and well-being as equally valuable]. World political reality is not very encouraging for those who adopt this egalitarian perspective. But then, unless one is beyond caring about our common future, there is no other sensible perspective available.'

Notes

1. C. Bergman (Ed.) (2003), *Another Day in Paradise: Front Line Stories from International Aid Workers*, Earthscan.
2. Reproduced in *The Guardian* Review, 11 October 2003, p34.
3. http://www.eveningtimes.co.uk/hi/news/5014367.html.
4. A detailed report by John Kampfner on the making of the Jessica Lynch story is available online at www.media.guardian.co.uk/broadcast/comment. The print version appeared in *The Guardian* on 15 May 2003.

References

Armes, R. (1974), *Film and Reality: A Historical Survey*, Penguin, Middlesex.

Corner, J., and K. Richardson (1986), 'Documentary meanings and the discourse of interpretation', in J. Corner (Ed.), *Documentary and the Mass Media*, Edward Arnold, London.

Chomsky, N. (1989), *Necessary Illusions*, South End Press, Boston.

Gripsrud, J. (2002), *Understanding Media Culture*, Arnold, London.

Hamelink, C. (1995), 'The democratic ideal and its enemies', in P. Lee (Ed.), *The Democratization of Communication*, University of Wales Press, Cardiff.

Herman, E. (1995), 'Media in the U.S. political economy', in J. Downing et al (Ed.), *Questioning the Media*, Sage, Thousand Oaks.

Kellner, D. (1995), *Media Culture: Cultural Studies, Identity and Politics Between the Modern and the Postmodern*, Routledge, London.

Minh-ha, T. (1993), 'The totalising quest for meaning', in M. Renov (Ed.), *Theorising Documentary*, Routledge, London.

Nordenstreng, K. (1995), 'The journalist: a walking paradox', in P. Lee (Ed.), *The Democratisation of Communication*, University of Wales Press, Cardiff.

Renov, M. (1993), 'Towards a poetics of documentary', in M. Renov (Ed.), *Theorising Documentary*, Arnold, London.

Silverstone, R. (1986), 'The agonistic narratives in television science', J. Corner (Ed.), *Documentary and the Mass Media*, Edward Arnold, London.

Wilson, T. (1993), *Watching Television: Hermeneutics, Reception, and Popular Culture*, Polity Press, Cambridge.

Three young women from Palestine

Patricia Holland

Private Jessica Lynch, from Palestine, West Virginia, was dramatically 'rescued' from the Iraqis by American forces, in a mission that was widely thought to be an event played up for the media. Rachel Corrie was a peace protestor with the International Solidarity Movement in the Gaza strip. She was killed by an Israeli bulldozer as she tried to prevent the demolition of Palestinian homes. Hiba Daraghmeh, born and brought up in Palestine, blew herself up in an Israeli shopping mall, killing four Israelis and wounding forty-eight. Each of these young women became an icon, but their images and their stories were circulated in very different ways.

This is the story of three young women whose photographs appeared in the media at the time of the second Iraq war. Newspapers print numerous photographs of young women. They add freshness and appeal to the pages and readers appreciate them – especially when they are attractive and smiling. In these days of instant celebrity *Big Brother* style, the likes of Victoria Beckham and Kylie Minogue share the pages with contestants from reality shows and others who just happen to be in the news. Life and celebrity run together, as posing, performance and high visibility become the order of the day. How you present yourself has a real importance in contemporary life, and looking attractive in a gossip magazine or a newspaper has definite appeal. The press, especially – but not only – the tabloids, need pictures of young women and there are plenty on offer.

It may seem that these observations are irrelevant when considering the reporting of the Middle East conflicts, but this is not so, for they provide the context within which women are routinely viewed in the British press, and femininity is put on show. Whatever the news story, if it involves a woman she will be the one who is pictured, and if the story centres on her, so much the better. There is a lingering feeling that pictures of beautiful women are, in the words of the *Sun* in 1984, 'a vital bit of cheer for readers depressed by strikes, deaths and disasters'.[1] So it happened that, during the Spring of 2003, amongst the pictured women were three young women from Palestine: a nineteen-year-old American soldier from Palestine, West Virginia; a twenty-three-year-old peace activist who travelled to Palestine in the Middle East; and a Palestinian student.

In the weeks of the second Gulf war, the front pages of the tabloids thundered with vivid explosions, camouflage clad troops, heavy armour and shattered victims, but the gossip pages, the lifestyle pages and the showbiz pages carried on much as always. This is an aspect of reporting a war which is all too often overlooked; however powerful a news report, however bloody a disaster or triumphant a victory, once it is placed within the well established domestic routines of the daily press, it is inevitably tamed and contained. Its effect is moderated by the familiar attitudes which inhabit the rest of the paper and which flow over into the war reporting itself. The daily press is, of its very nature, committed to variety; including news stories of all sorts, the trivial as well as the significant, and gossip, human interest and entertainment as well as information. The smiling young women in the news pages have much in common with the smiling young women in those other richly illustrated sections. Rather than deploring this phenomenon of news as pot-pourri (deplorable though it may frequently be), I am suggesting that we should take a cool look at the overlap between the focus of the news and the background noise against which it is received. Critiques of war reporting usually concentrate on hard facts and set out to expose inaccuracies and distortion, but it is equally important to study the cultural climate in which the information is (like many of the war reporters) embedded.

At the same time we should look out for the ways in which news and information sidestepped the familiar routines of the conventional news media and avoided their ready made attitudes. These alternative media ranged from the age old methods of posters and pamphlets, to the contemporary expansion of the Internet. Email groups could circulate letters, notes, contact addresses and significant articles; weblogs posted the diaries of individuals at the centre of the action.

In narratives of war, the gap between the genders tends to widen and the roles assigned to women tend to become more passive and limited. 'Women and children' quickly become archetypal victims, while masculinity takes on a harder edge. This was amply illustrated in the language and imagery of the popular press at the time of the Falklands War, when *Express* columnist Peter McKay crowed,

> Cut the girl talk. This is war ... Men like to fight and are excited by the prospect of battle ... Perhaps in response to these times when men walk tall, tap-room Pattons arrange task forces in sausage dishes and women keep quiet, there has in the past few days been a small outbreak of nostalgia for men as brutes ... Right now it must be quite hard to be a feminist (30 April 1982).[2]

But women have always had a highly complex relationship to war. This is now much less easy to dismiss, partly due to those very feminists sneered at by Peter McKay, and also due to the inexorable rise of women war correspondents who have refused to ignore the active part played by the women they observe. Said the BBC's chief news correspondent, Kate Adie, 'I've never been in a single riot or war or other dangerous situation where half the people present weren't female. Who is providing food, clearing up, looking after the victims, consoling the relatives? It's always women'.[3] Those traditional roles of consolation, support and reconstruction have taken on a new, dynamic significance in reporting such as Adie's, and at the same time women have pushed into the heart of the action. By the first Gulf War a significant number of soldiers were women. 'Mum's off to battle' was the caption of one picture in which a soldier kisses goodbye to her seven-week-old baby (*Today*, 28 August 1990), while Saddam Hussein was said to have been outraged by the numbers of women in shorts tramping over his country. The three young women I am concerned with all took decisive action in a non-traditional way. They were women doing 'unwomanly' things, but, in each case, their femininity became an issue, constraining the possibilities of their independent action and ultimately determining the ways in which their image and their stories were circulated and used.

Jessica Lynch was a supply clerk with a non-combat unit of the American army who became a household name when she was rescued from captivity in Iraq and returned to her home in West Virginia. Rachel Corrie was an American volunteer with the international movement that aimed to show solidarity with the Palestinian people. She was killed when an Israeli army bulldozer ran over her as she took part in a protest against the demolition of homes in the Gaza strip. Hiba Daraghmeh was born and brought up in Palestine – although that country does not officially exist. She blew herself up in an Israeli shopping mall, killing four Israelis and wounding forty-eight. All three women gained an iconic status. All three had made choices which put their very lives at risk, and all three had their image and their stories used in ways which sometimes seemed strangely detached from the reality of those lives.

These disparate stories, which link the long running Arab/Israeli conflict to the US-led invasion of Iraq, were circulated in strikingly different ways. Private Jessica became an American heroine. Pictures of her dramatic rescue were played repeatedly on US television; there were 'America loves Jessica' fridge magnets, stickers, T-shirts and mugs; and the governor of West Virginia planned to declare a 'Jessica Lynch day'. As the princess at the centre of a fairy-tale rescue story, she also symbolised homely American values and humanised American power. In the *Observer*, Lawrence Donnegan argued that the 'simple yet powerful narrative of American redemption' changed the public mood in the US, which had been faltering in its support of the war (6 April 2003).

Rachel Corrie was far less visible in the mainstream media, particularly in the US. After all, she had been demonstrating against US interests. In Britain her death earned small paragraphs in the tabloids, but there was longer and more thoughtful comment in the broadsheets. She gained her celebrity chiefly through alternative media, web sites, email groups and the growing International Solidarity Movement (ISM) which recruited volunteers for the increasingly dangerous mission of support in Palestine. Photographs show demonstrating Palestinian children holding up posters with Rachel's portrait, and her picture also appeared on a booklet published by the ISM, ('Israel, stop killing the peace'). A Canadian MP nominated the ISM for a Nobel peace prize in recognition of Rachel and other activists who had been wounded. Hiba Daraghmeh's suicide mission made her a heroine, too, but this time it was amongst militants committed to violence rather than peace activists. After her death she, too, had her picture reproduced on a poster – published by Islamic Jihad, the radical organisation that had begun to recruit women as suicide bombers.

Women are constantly under scrutiny, and their appearance and clothing has particular significance. British newspapers carried family portraits of Jessica and Rachel, typical of the smiling young women who are routinely dispersed through the pages. The two were strikingly similar; both long-haired, blonde and smooth-skinned, with that crafted perfection of the classic American teenager. Rachel wears sunglasses on her head, a relaxed expression and a light scarf around her neck. Jessica has clear blue eyes, a wispy fringe, and a look that declares 'I'm having my photo taken'. But a picture that was used more frequently shows her in army uniform. Here her long hair is pulled back, her camouflage cap is pulled firmly on to her head and her smile is confident. She poses in front of the stars and stripes.

Cynthia Enloe has described how, from the early days of women's recruitment into the armed forces, the authorities have striven to protect their femininity while integrating them into the masculine ethos of the force.[4] This has meant that they must have a uniform that is neither too masculine – which would reduce the all-important difference between women and men – nor too feminine – which would undermine male camaraderie and the fighting ethic. One US 1940s recruiting poster reconciled the dilemma by insisting, 'Some of the best soldiers wear lipstick'. (A newer generation of action heroines from Linda Hamilton to Lara Croft has shifted the perception of fighting women – they are not in uniform and their femininity is excessive rather than the reverse.) But the uniform has another significance. Whatever the gender of its wearer, it legitimates violence. The reports of Jessica's rescue included accounts of her capture by Iraqi soldiers, in which she was described as 'fighting them to the death'. One US military official 'described a scene in which the nineteen-year-old recruit fired her weapon until she ran out of ammunition, killing several enemy soldiers' (*Observer* 6 April). Her vulnerable femininity and her reported aggression could both be encapsulated in the legitimising uniform and the narrative of rescue.

Hiba wears a uniform of a different sort. During her lifetime she was described as hiding from public view, concealing her face as well as her body with her Muslim veil. Her family tells how her gradual move towards a more fundamentalist Islam was reflected in a more extreme form of Islamic dress. Her fellow students say they had only ever seen her eyes, and she was described as always avoiding the company of men. Her dress – which emphasised her femaleness even as it set out to conceal her femininity – indicated a belief system that justified the deadly aggression that she herself could not survive. Her 'disguise' was to wear western clothing – some reports speak of jeans, others of high heels and a miniskirt – as she approached the security check at the shopping mall where she detonated her explosives. After her death her face was not only revealed, but also made publicly available on a poster – published, ironically, by that very fundamentalist group who believe strongly that women should cover themselves. The group also published a pamphlet on their website and circulated it in the universities in the West Bank and the Gaza Strip praising its women fighters, who 'have exchanged their perfume for the smell of the land and wear weapons on their arms instead of jewellery' (*Associated Press*, 31 May 2003). To them Hiba was a martyr, but to Israel and the Western media, she was a terrorist. The day after the bombing, the Israeli authorities dynamited her parents' home. In response her family plastered onto the rubble a copy of the poster displaying her secret face.

Of the three women, Rachel had the greatest freedom to select her own clothing, and, in life, to control her own image. The front page of the *Guardian's* tabloid section, G2 (18 March) shows her – or perhaps it is another demonstrator – as, no doubt, she would have wanted to be seen. (The picture, taken by one of the ISM volunteers, is not credited in the *Guardian*, and the paper does not make it clear whether this actually is Rachel. As she was part of a group who was acting together, this does not matter very much.) The picture shows the back of a young woman in a day-glo jacket shouting through a megaphone at a bulldozer that menaces the camera as well as the protestor. Its lights are shining; there is a shadowy figure at the wheel and bent metal in the foreground. In all the accounts of Rachel's death she is described as wearing a bright orange jacket such as those worn by workers on railway tracks, building sites and other dangerous places. Far from legitimising aggression, this symbolic clothing – common to men and women – warns that the wearer should be looked out for and kept safe. In this case it was also intended to show that this is a non-violent demonstrator, someone who is specifically *not* in uniform. (Although the Israeli army claimed that the bulldozer operator did not see her (*Guardian*, 3 May)). Rachel was less constrained by her femininity than either of the other two women, but here she was playing the traditional female role of peace-maker. But she was consciously playing it in a highly dangerous way. Unlike Hiba with her explosives and Jessica with her army rifle, she carried no weapon. Her only protection from the Israeli forces was the moral protection given by her orange jacket, her nationality and her femininity. She was present to prevent a violent act, rather than to commit one, and she was also present as a highly visible witness, ensuring that the Israeli actions were not kept secret and warning the Israelis of the adverse publicity that would follow from harming an American woman. By contrast with the other two, she was not fighting for her country, but was part of a demonstration *against* her country and its client, Israel. In her orange jacket, sponsored by an unofficial international organisation, she had moved beyond the additional protection that nationhood and uniform could have offered.

News of her death came on 17 March, just three days before the attack on Iraq began. A group of four British and four American volunteers had been trying to block two bulldozers which were destroying homes and farming infrastructure near an olive grove. Since the autumn of 2001, Israel had begun to occupy tracts of the territory nominally under the control of the Palestinian authority in the West Bank and the Gaza Strip, and, claiming reprisals for suicide bombings and other attacks, were systematically bulldozing Palestinian homes and farming land. The International Solidarity Movement had been created to support the Palestinian people and help them reconstruct their homes and their lives, but, as the invasions occurred, its members increasingly found themselves acting as 'human shields'. There were many eyewitnesses to Rachel's death and the news reports quoted several different protesters who had been present. Nineteen-year-old Nicholas Duric told the *Independent*,

> We were trying to frustrate their efforts by getting in front of the bulldozers ... One of the drivers saw Rachel and drove towards her. She didn't get out of the way and he didn't stop. She was carried up with a heap of earth in the shovel of the bulldozer. The driver continued working. She slipped and fell and was run over by the bulldozer. The driver saw that she had fallen but carried her along for another sixteen feet. Only then did he back off (17 March).

Another witness described him as driving back over Rachel's body. Later Rachel's father explained that he had himself driven bulldozers, but that this one was 'a sixty-ton behemoth especially designed by [the American company] Caterpillar for house demolitions, a far bigger machine than anything he had ever seen or driven'.[5] Comparing the US response to Jessica's rescue with that of Rachel's death, Naomi Klein noted 'the lives of some US citizens, even young, beautiful white women, are valued more than others' (*Guardian* 22 May).

Jessica's life was indeed highly valued as a propaganda tool for the US government. Three days into the war, she had been in a US supply convoy that had been ambushed by Iraqi troops. An unknown number of soldiers were killed, and at least five were taken captive. Pictures of the bodies were shown on Iraqi television, and the American prisoners – who also included a woman, Shoshana Johnson, a black cook – were publicly questioned. They replied tentatively and appeared terrified. This display was greeted with outrage in the Western media. It was described as 'parading' – the word was universally used – and it was seen as quite different from the pictures of captured Iraqis routinely shown on British and US networks – often in extremely humiliating circumstances. (Jon Snow, of *Channel Four News*, described how the outcry had caused his programme to take advice on the legality of showing prisoners at all. C4 news was told that no international conventions covered television in this way.)[6] Jessica's pictures were made available by the US authorities and the *Sun* reported on 'The first girl lost in the war' (25 March).

Then, at 3am on 2 April, a news conference was called at the press centre in Qatar ('we thought they'd caught Saddam Hussein or something' said one correspondent) to announce her rescue. The tone was triumphant and the story was illustrated with clips from impressive night-sight video footage taken by the military. The next day the UK tabloids took up the story with some dynamic double page spreads using juxtapositions, dramatic headlines and visuals of different textures and origins. In several papers the centrepiece was a snatched frame of Jessica's face on a stretcher, caught as her eyes momentarily engage with the camera: 'the bright smile of the young recruit is rekindled as Jessica is carried from the hospital', captioned the *Express*. There were inset pictures of Jessica's family and friends in her home town; line drawings and diagrams to enhance the drama. The *Express* used a comic strip sequence, liberally sprinkled with dramatically blazing guns, helicopters, heavy armour and collapsing enemy soldiers in vaguely oriental gear. Blurry night-vision circular frames showed the rescuing group rushing towards a helicopter. The headline 'Saving Private Lynch' was irresistible. Jim Wilkinson, the US army spokesman, was quoted as saying 'America does not leave its heroes behind – never has, never will'.

But although she was a hero, and despite her ability to 'kill several Iraqi soldiers', the story recreated the classic gender relations of war. There were the 'delta force commandos with blacked-up faces and night vision goggles' (*Express*) who 'opened fire as soon as they hit the ground' (*Sun*); the enemy who is both dangerous and fanatical, and the vulnerable young woman rescued from a hospital which was 'used as a base by Saddam Hussein's death squads' (*Sun*) and had 'become the HQ of "chemical Ali" '. 'Her rescuers found her manacled to a bed next to equipment that could have been used in torture' (*Mail*). (The anti-war *Mirror* took the opportunity to juxtapose an account of a US missile that had killed passers-by near a Baghdad maternity hospital. An Iraqi mother 'wounded in the checkpoint blitz that killed eleven members of her family, said "I saw the heads of my two little girls come off"'.)

From the start, the heavy hand of news management could easily be detected. For the more sceptical parts of the British press Jessica's story was already 'suspiciously heart-warming'. 'If it isn't immediately optioned by a film studio I'll consume an entire platoon of tanks' wrote Kathryn Flett (*Observer*, 6 April). In fact, when the BBC's *Correspondent* team visited the hospital, it was revealed that there were no soldiers present for the commandos to fight; that this was a bona fide hospital; that Jessica had been cared for and that the staff had tried to return her to the US military days before the 'rescue' – but the ambulance had been fired on by the Americans. One of the doctors told *Correspondent* that the rescuers behaved as if they had been making an action movie, 'with jumping and shouting, breaking the door', and all of it 'with the photos'. *Correspondent* pointed out that several bodies of American soldiers were recovered in the raid, and 'a bad story was turned into a good one'.[7]

The femininity of Hiba Daraghmeh was challenged and exploited in a quite different way. In many ways her story appeared alien to a Western readership. If Rachel fitted the established image of women peace protesters and Jessica that of the Hollywood heroine, Hiba was the subject of long lasting orientalism in Western reporting of Islam, which refuses to understand the history and context of actions.[8] First, she was seen as a terrorist, a fanatical suicide bomber, and secondly, as a fundamentalist, a devout Muslim woman, who accepted that her movements should be restricted and her body concealed. And yet that very difference from Western manners needs to be seen as part of the relationship that links the new fundamentalisms and the West. After all, Hiba was reported to be a student – not of Koranic studies, but of English Literature. The Iranian historian Homa Nategh has described how, in Iran during the last years of the Shah's regime, 'the chador reappeared in student circles as a sign of protest against westernisation and imperialism' and such was the feeling against the Shah and his Western backers that women shouted 'Khomeini, order me to shed the blood of others'.[9] Similarly, amongst Palestinians in the refugee camps, when the disciplined political organisation of the resistance movement was undermined in the 1980s, 'women ... discarded the secular "look" associated with the Resistance period (T-shirts and jeans) for long-sleeved dresses and headscarves. Women's conversation became heavily loaded with invocations of God's compassion and power'.[10] Hiba's mission was reported to have 'raised something of a feminist debate amongst Palestinians: should women hop over conservative societal barriers and join the almost exclusively male ranks of suicide bombers?'[11]

The image of a woman wrapped in black is not survival from the past, but a contemporary phenomenon.[12] Nevertheless as part of a Western orientalist fantasy, it has been a curious component of the presentation of the Iraqi war. Kate Adie's assertion that many women are visible in war has not been reflected in the television coverage of the Iraqi conflict, where the streets are crowded with men and women are only glimpsed as dark figures in the background. There has been little attempt to seek out women, to record their views, or even to draw attention to their absence. From time to time there has been a snatched television interview, and one can sense the sexual titillation as news cameramen (and they are almost all men) attempt to glimpse the hidden faces. 'Where are the Iraqi women?' asked Natasha Walter in the *Guardian*, pointing out that the Iraqi leaders selected by the US had (at the time when she was writing) included only one woman (25 April). As resistance to the occupiers grows, much of it organised – as in Iran and Palestine – around fundamentalist Islam, the position of women becomes more precarious. Even Channel Four's magnificent correspondent Lindsay Hilsum explained that she would not have been allowed to interview Shi'ia men in Basra unless she had put a scarf over her head (25 June 2003). A rare *Newsnight* item on the position of women pointed out that many women are now afraid to go out without their Islamic dress (BBC2, 2 July).

In real life the three women I have been discussing were exercising what choices they could. Hiba was clearly under tremendous pressure, a nineteen-year-old who had spent her life amongst a shattered community, 'a child of the Palestinian intifada' (*Independent*, 21 May). Although she was educated, the future must have appeared totally blank. She may have shared the view of the female Jihad activist who told the Associated Press reporter that, 'as a Palestinian living in Nablus … she already risks being killed by a random stray bullet. She said she would rather be a suicide bomber so that she can "take them [Israelis] with me to the grave"' (31 May 2003). Jessica came from a tiny Appalachian farming community. America may be prosperous, but in Palestine, West Virginia, unemployment is twenty per cent. She, too had limited options. '"The military is the one good chance of getting an education and making something of themselves"', said a cousin (*Sun*, 25 March). Rachel was educated, comfortably off and had many possibilities open to her. She chose to act in solidarity with those less fortunate.

When we compare the ways in which these three stories were used, it is clear that the image of Jessica was the least related to her own self-presentation. She was used as a propaganda tool for the US, and in the process was completely silenced. She has not given her own account of her capture, nor of her treatment at the hands of the Iraqis, nor her view of her rescuers. No interview with her has been published or recorded. *Correspondent* was told she had no memory of the whole episode 'and probably never will'. However, she *was* invited to join the world of celebrity and entertainment. A letter from CBS television was leaked to the *New York Times*, inviting her to host a music video programme on MTV2.[13]

Both Rachel and Hiba were active agents for whom visibility was part of the aim. The destruction wrought by Hiba was partly vengeance for loss of life in the Palestinian territories, and partly a public demonstration of a last ditch, desperate form of resistance. But she, too, could not speak on her own behalf, prevented by the paradox in which the only radical ideology available to her was one which silenced women. Rachel was the only one of the women whose own words were heard. In the long, articulate emails she sent to her family, later published by the *Guardian* and the ISM, she describes how her time was spent largely with Palestinian women and families. After her death, her mother took up her cause – appealing to women in America and the Middle East and vowing to continue Rachel's witness.[14]

To conclude, as the stories of these three young women show, when we look at the media in times of war, it is not just the reporting of an event that we should be considering, but the creation and circulation of mythologies and imagery. As Sharon Macdonald has written, 'to consider the imagery of women in peace and war is to face arguments about the very nature of the sexes and of human needs and instincts.'[15] At the same time, by looking at the context of the news, and by picking up hints and putting together details and passing references, we can begin to create a space in which those who have been so rapidly labelled then left behind as events move on can begin to be understood from their own perspective.

Acknowledgement

Thanks to Matt Holland (no relation) of Bournemouth University Library, for help with sources.

Notes

1. Quoted in Patricia Holland, 'The politics of the smile: "soft news" and the sexualisation of the popular press', Cynthia Carter et al (Eds), *News, Gender and Power*, Routledge, London, 1998.
2. Discussed in Patricia Holland, 'In these times when men walk tall: the popular press and the Falklands Conflict', *Cencrastus*, Edinburgh, 1982.
3. Quoted by Anne Sebba, *Battling For the News: The Rise of the Woman Reporter*, Hodder and Stoughton, London, 1994, p.272. See also Kate Adie, *The Kindness of Strangers*, Headline, London, 2002.
4. Cynthia Enloe, *Does Khaki Become You? The Militarisation of Women's Lives*, Pluto, London, 1983.
5. www.counterpunch.org/said.
6. *The True Face of War*, Channel Four, 5 June 2003.
7. *Correspondent: War Spin*, BBC2, 18 May 2003.
8. Edward Said, *Covering Islam: How the Media and the Experts Determine How We See the Rest of the World*, Vintage, London, 1981/1997.
9. Homa Nategh, 'Women: the damned of the Iranian revolution', Rosemary Ridd and

Helen Callaway (Eds), *Caught up in Conflict:Women's Responses to Political Strife*, Macmillan, Basingstoke, 1986, pp56 and 47.

10. Rosemary Sayigh, and Julie Peteet, 'Between two fires: Palestinian women in Lebanon,' in Ridd and Callaway, *op cit*, p128.

11. Associated Press, 31 May 2003.

12. John Gray, *Al-Qaeda and What is Means to be Modern*, Faber and Faber, London, 2003.

13. John Willis, 'A warning from America', *Broadcast*, 4 July 2003. Despite US Army doctors continuing to insist that Jessica Lynch is unlikely to recover her memory of her experiences in Iraq, she has signed a $1 million book deal for her memoirs, entitled 'I am a soldier, too: the Jessica Lynch story'. It is to be written by Rick Bragg, a journalist who resigned from the *New York Times* after it was revealed that his reports had been written by a trainee (*Guardian*, 3 September 2003).

14. Cindy Corrie's statement can be found at http://www.counterpunch.org/corrie.

15. Sharon Macdonald, Pat Holden, and Shirley Ardener, *Images of Women in Peace and War; Cross-cultural and Historical Perspectives*, Macmillan, Basingstoke, 1987, p3.

Innocent victims/active citizens: children and media war coverage

Máire Messenger Davies

This article looks at the ways in which images of children are used to arouse emotions in adult audiences, and to illustrate news agendas in which children themselves often have no active part. The article discusses recent research with primary schoolchildren, which indicates that eleven- and twelve-year-olds are capable of commenting on and drawing inferences from adult news coverage in ways that indicate considerable political sophistication. Children object to their own representation as passive victims, and assert their right to 'have their voices heard.' [1]

Introduction

The cover of the G2 section of *The Guardian* of 8 August 2003 consists of a full-page picture of the head and shoulders of a small boy, with his head bandaged, his fearful eyes turned upwards towards the camera, and his lips pressed together, as if he were trying not to cry. From the top left hand corner of the picture a hand presses a gauze pad against his face. The skin on the visible part of his torso is pitted with abscesses and part of his chest is covered in white foam. He has two white-bandaged stumps where his arms should be. The headline is 'Remember Ali? Esther Addley on what happened next.'

Addley's G2 story described how Ali Ismaeel Abbas, an eleven-year-old Iraqi boy injured in a bomb attack on Baghdad in April 2003, 'will fly to the UK next week to be fitted for prosthetic arms and begin up to six months of physiotherapy.' She comments: 'It is an extraordinarily happy ending for the little boy whose doctors at one point told journalists "it would be better if he died."' The use of the phrase 'happy ending' reveals the narrative structure of Ali's 'story'. Ali is not just a 'story' but a reassuring story. He is also, Addley points out, an 'iconic figure'; the inside page of G2 has a charming recent photograph of him, curly-haired and smooth-complexioned, kissing one of his stumps. To create this 'happy story', tabloid newspapers, like intrepid explorers, 'beat a path' to his bed; emotional newspaper appeals for the public to pay for treatment were launched. The Australian Peter Wilson, who 'got him out of Baghdad' is the unacknowledged 'hero' of the story (not Tony Blair as had been claimed) and, thanks to the generosity of the public, Ali will be treated in Kuwait for as long as he needs to be.

But all this is only part of Ali's 'story'; fourteen members of his family, including both his parents, were killed in the attack that injured him. Ali has become (for the time being – as long as he remains an attractive child) a tabloid icon. But he no longer has a social context: he has lost his family, he has been removed from his country, and through this process he has become divorced from the wider political and moral context of the war itself. His horrific injuries which, according to Addley, made the Gulf bureau chief of Reuters weep, are no longer an instance of the viciousness of war, and thus a potential reminder of its immorality; he has become a human interest story, with 'a happy ending'. Looked at from a wider perspective, Ali's 'story' even becomes insignificant: he and his family are just a small fraction of the several thousand Iraqi civilians who have been killed or injured in a war whose legitimacy and effectiveness continue to be challenged – a story which has by no means ended, happily or otherwise. Ali may be a 'story'; but the question is, what kind of story? And whose?

Research background

This essay considers the use made of children, like Ali, in media coverage of war and traumatic events. The essay draws on work from two research projects in which the author has recently been involved – one, published in 2001, funded by the Broadcasting Standards Commission, about the use of children in non-fiction adult television, the other an ongoing study on children and television news. The BSC research examined whether children gave, or were able to give, their informed consent to the different ways in which they were represented in adult television shows. This research arose from a number of complaints made by viewers to the BSC about the 'abuse' of children, for example, being made to compete in adult game shows, or being reduced to tears in a *Panorama* interview about adoption. The question we addressed in this research was whether children's consent had been sought for these representations, and what were the ways in which adult institutions dealing with children (such as the law and the media) try to establish whether children were capable of giving informed consent. (In the media, the answer to this is far from clear.[2]) The second project, on children and news, is more specifically related to war; it arose from an interest in the coverage of 11 September 2001 and its aftermath by children's news programmes. This was the topic of a conference organised by the broadcasting consumer group, the Voice of the Listener and Viewer, in November 2001.[3]

From discussions with the children's news producers at this conference, it became clear that we had areas of common interest, particularly our interest in children's potential capacity to understand and respond to news stories about war and disaster, and (in the case of my research) to give informed consent to their own representation in adult programming. Both the producers and I, from our different perspectives, operated from an assumption that children need to be treated as intelligent potential citizens when considering news coverage of traumatic events, especially those involving children themselves – although consideration always had to be given to the possibility of distress and incomprehension. These considerations are necessary both for producers and for researchers working with children on sensitive topics. From the conference presentations by children's news producers – Matthew Price of the BBC's *Newsround*, Lea Sellers and Maddy Wilshire of the Channel 4 Schools news programme, *First Edition*, and Ben Thomas of S4C's Welsh language children's news bulletin, *Ffeil* – it appeared that children's news producers gave more attention to the possible impact of their stories and presentations on their audiences than did adult producers. They were particularly concerned to provide explanatory context and background and, again unlike adult news, they saw their service as interactive – inviting children to write to them, to send emails and to contribute to websites, which in turn fed back into their construction of stories. A conception of the child audience as interactive participants in the construction and interpretation of current affairs informed these producers' attitude to the use of children, both as presenters and as viewers, in their programmes. This is also a view of children that researchers with children implicitly take when they interview or survey them, although it is not always made explicit. Children are not just objects of research; they are subjects, and the importance of children's reflexivity – getting them to comment on their own participation – had emerged from our research with children and families in *Consenting Children?* and also from earlier work on a BBC-funded study on children and broadcasting.[4]

The producers of Channel 4's news programme for Schools, *First Edition*, Lea Sellers and Maddy Wilshire, talked at the conference about letters they had received from children in response to their programme, and they allowed me and my colleagues at Cardiff and UWE, Bristol (with the consent of the children and their schools) to have access to these letters. From this, a number of research initiatives have been launched by our research group,[5] one of which is a British Academy funded archive of *First Edition* tapes, scripts and papers, including the children's letters, kindly donated by the producers when the programme ceased production in early 2003.[6] (See also Cynthia Carter, in this issue[7].) The work described in this essay is part of these ongoing initiatives.

Children's functions in news

Ali is a particularly clear example of the ways in which children serve certain specific functions in news coverage of war and disaster – not all of these functions being in the child's broader interests, and often (because a child may be sick or unconscious) without the child's explicit consent. In the rest of this essay, I want to look more closely at some of the ways in which representations of children were used in the recent coverage of the Iraqi war in March-April 2003, including news bulletins in the period during the lead-up to war. I then want to discuss some examples of children's own comments on the way in which children are featured in the news, including the representation of war, drawn from questionnaires, letters and interviews with the primary school children in Glasgow who regularly wrote to *First Edition*.

The goal of this discussion is to begin to try to integrate media representations of 'the child as object' with comments from actual children about the ways in which children are *represented* as objects. Through these comments, I want to draw attention to the ways in which children constitute themselves as subjects and as agents, which is a function of citizenship. The broader context of these analyses is a theoretical concern with contemporary constructions of childhood (see e.g. James and Prout, 1997[8]) which seek to contest the Romantic notion of the child as 'innocent', 'becoming', and 'incompetent'. Within this broad field of childhood studies, there are a number of specific studies about actual children and their competence – particularly their competence as 'citizens', that is, as active agents within their own societies. A number of scholars have looked at this question empirically with regard to children's relationship with the media, for example, Buckingham and the present author, and this research is part of this ongoing examination.[9]

Features of children's media representation

One aspect of our concern is the ways in which children are used, not as active participants, but for signification purposes in the media. In the *Consenting Children?* project, we did an analysis of a sample of broadcast output over two days and identified three main characteristics of the ways in which children were used in adult television programmes: (i) Passivity (Illustration); (ii) Entertainment; and (iii) Emotionalism.[10] Our sample of programming came from the terrestrial broadcasting channels on 27-28 October 2000 in which we identified a total of 55 child-related sequences – between 12 per cent and 13 per cent of the material recorded. These were categorised according to genre and/or targeted audience. By far the greatest number of child-related items were Advertisements (60 per cent) and the next most frequent category was News (20 per cent). 15 per cent of the sample was classified as Children's programmes; and 'General programming' (including family programmes, adult entertainment such as dramas, comedy shows, talk shows) comprised the rest of the sample.

The role played by children

Apart from the obvious role of the use of children in advertisements in order to sell products, which we did not discuss, it was possible to identify the three main characteristics of the use of children in all these various genres – passivity, entertainment and emotion. Passivity and emotionalism were particular characteristics of the way in which children were portrayed in news, and I will focus on these here.

Passivity

We defined 'passivity' as a lack of participation of the child in the events; images were used to illustrate a subject, when children were the topic of debate, but the children had no intervention in it. They were not interviewed, and were not shown as central to any activity that was going on. There are many examples of this kind of use of children in the war coverage discussed below. Passivity also arises from a lack of agency (ability to control the action) – even if some form of participation is allowed. In our BSC study, this happened with game shows where, despite the fact that children were the competitors, all the circumstances of their participation were controlled by the producers and the presenters of the programme. Such forms of passivity were occasionally noted in my analysis of war coverage (see below.)

In the 20 per cent of the programme sample which came into the News category, several items specifically referred to children: there were stories on the early release of the child murderers of the toddler James Bulger; on the BSE inquiry; on an appeal made by the Duke of York against child cruelty; on a toy fair; and on British schools failing black students. Most of the items (unusually) concerned a subject related to children, but in none of them was the child an active agent. For example, in the first ITV news at 5.30 am on 27 October 2000, the BSE inquiry was illustrated with images of fourteen-year-old Zoe Jeffries infected with CJD, the BSE human variant, lying paralysed in bed, accompanied by two other young girls, in what was obviously an attempt to appeal to viewers' emotions. The children in this item were not given any part to play, and obviously the sick girl could not have given her consent; their images were simply used as illustrative of a news item about the broader issue of BSE.

Emotionalism

Children are used in this way to appeal to adults' feelings and to influence their views. Charity advertisements to aid African countries, for example, tend to make use of images of children in need of urgent aid as a direct and easy way to appeal to compassion and solidarity, often replacing the necessity to provide deeper explanations of the cultural, economic, and political realities behind the crises. The story of how Ali (minus the fourteen members of his family) was treated by the media is a good example of this strategy. Readers (including politicians) are enabled to relieve some of their concerns about the possible immorality of war in general and this war in particular, by being helped to feel that they are at least contributing to one child's rehabilitation. The rehabilitation of children is always more appealing than the rehabilitation of the adult injured – as is the case with discharged soldiers for instance, many of whom may end up homeless or in trouble with the law. Their cases are not as amenable to 'happy ending' narratives as those of photogenic eleven-year-olds.

Children as 'monsters'; children as 'innocents'

Our *Consenting Children?* analysis indicated a duality in the ways in which children are represented in the media: on the one hand, there is the innocent child who is allowed to play adult-like roles for the sake of entertainment or who is an innocent victim of a disaster like a bomb attack or BSE; on the other, there is the controversial child who is of interest to the audience because of his/her 'evil' nature, such as children who kill. Both the 'innocent' and the 'evil' can be found in representations of children at war, often combined in the same children – as has happened with stories covering the child warriors of Liberia. Are they war criminals or victims? News reporters find it difficult to present 'stories' that could possibly have 'happy endings' about such children because of the duality of their roles.

The coverage of the war in Iraq

The School of Journalism, Media and Cultural Studies has been video-recording news programmes from all the terrestrial TV channels and from Sky News for the last year. The initial object of this recording was to analyse stories for a research project about asylum seekers. When the war with Iraq seemed imminent, colleagues in JOMEC received funding from the BBC to use these tapes to analyse war coverage.[11] The existence of these recordings also permitted our children and news research team to analyse some of the news items with regard to their use of children.

For the purpose of this essay, I took a small sample of news from the BBC and ITN 6pm and 10pm bulletins on 4 and 5 December 2002; 25 February 2003; and 28 March 2003. These bulletins included local news on the BBC but not on ITV. The December and February news items were prior to the war; the March items were during it.

The sample consisted of 156 news items altogether. Of the 83 wartime items, including local news (28 March), 61 (over 73 per cent) were war-related.

My concern in establishing how children were represented and used in these news items was twofold:

(i)   How many stories featured children at all?
(ii) In what capacities, in terms of agency, passivity and emotionalism, were children featured?

Out of the 156 items, there were 47 (30 per cent) representations of children altogether: a 'representation' was any reference at all to a child or children, whether verbal or visual, and I included references to young people (teenagers) in my definition. An example of a verbal reference was a report of a vicar charged with child sex abuse. An example of a visual representation was a shot of children sleeping in a community centre after their homes were threatened by fire in Australia. Of the 22 (30 per cent) out of 73 stories in the pre-war December bulletins which featured children, only two had any connection with the impending war: both occurred in the BBC 10pm bulletin on 25 February, 2003; one, from Egypt, showed a small boy on a man's shoulders yelling in protest, the other showed a close-up of a child accompanying her mother in a war protest in the UK (tight close-ups, an emotive technique, are a common feature of televisual representations of children). Other items included news about students demonstrating against university fees; Michael Jackson dangling his baby son over a balcony; children and their families fleeing fires in Australia; and a fatal accident on a school bus in South Wales, in which a twelve-year-old boy was killed. It is obvious from this small sample, that although regular news items have a tendency to feature children in stories which are about accidents or disaster, most of these stories were directly about children themselves, whether as victims of accidents or of eccentric parenting or of callous governments. Only in one of these examples – the Australian fires story – were children used as incidental illustrations – i.e. 'passively' and 'emotionally' – in the shot of families sheltering in a community centre. In the other items, children/young people were actively featured speaking about their lost schoolfriend (in the accident story) and about the difficulties of student debt (the fees story). In these cases, they appeared as agents.

In my analysis of wartime stories, children disappear as active agents. 27 of the

83 wartime stories featured children and 19 (over 70 per cent of the 27) were war-related. I classified these stories according to whether the children were used:

(i)   'Passively' – that is, as having no role other than background;

(ii) 'Passively/Illustratively' to underline a point being made by the reporter (for example, close-ups of infants lying limply in their anxious mothers' arms as a refugee group got caught in military crossfire);

(iii) 'Actively', that is being the actual subject of a news item;

(iv) 'Actively/Illustratively', that is being shown taking an active role (for instance a small boy shouting anti-American slogans) but only to illustrate a wider point about Iraqi resistance to the invasion.

Among these 27 items, there was only one example of children/young people being active agents – the war protesters, mentioned above. Ironically, their way of protesting was to be passive: to lie down in the road and to pretend to be dead. All other examples of the use of children were Passive or Passive/Illustrative. Children were shown as 'patients' both in the grammatical and medical sense; depicted as being on the receiving end of other people's actions, including being injured, and being medically treated. There was no footage of dead children, presumably arising from the news convention (comprehensively breached in the case of Saddam Hussein's sons) that to show footage of dead people is a mark of disrespect. While this may be the case, this convention certainly underestimates the true impact of war on children. And, once a child is dead, there is no possibility of heart-warming stories with 'happy endings'. The majority of visual representations in the war-story sample emphasised this overwhelming sense of passivity by showing children either lying down; being carried; or being held by the hand. No child spoke on camera. The same footage was used by both BBC and ITN, and it was used for both the early and late bulletins. The repeated image of childhood here was one of persistent victimhood and lack of autonomy, with, in just one or two examples, an image of unruly, rebellious boyhood. Girls were not shown in even these limited active roles at all.

'Tory Tony WILL NOT CHANGE MY MIND': children as active agents

> George Bush said: 'This is a war against global terrorism'. – This is a war against a dictator run and led by terrorists. Tony can't improve our transport, invest in our NHS or even give fire-fighters £30K a year each – but, ah, he can put aside a healthy £5.5 BILLION for a war. MADNESS as the Mirror said.
>
> 11 year old boy, Glasgow, letter to *First Edition* (emphases in original).

From their representation in media coverage, it seems that children are not seen as having any active role to play in war news coverage. Their images serve the purpose of arousing horror (but not too much horror) and pity, but their voices are not heard.[12] This kind of coverage ignores the necessity of informed consent as identified in our BSC research on the use of children in factual programming. Furthermore, *pace* the Government's emphasis on the citizenship curriculum in UK schools, nowhere in all this is any evidence of 'citizens in the making', as both Buckingham and Davies (ibid) call them.

As the producers of *First Edition* reasoned in both showing and consulting children in their war coverage, wartime especially is an occasion for mobilising the political awareness and consciences of the young. Our research with primary school children suggests that they are not satisfied with a representation of themselves and their contemporaries in the media as innocent victims, grateful for adult intervention when they suffer horrific injuries, otherwise silently lying in the background while soldiers and embedded journalists do the real work of war and its reporting, and then dying off-camera later. Furthermore, the children we have interviewed have views on media coverage and news agendas which range more widely than the war itself; their responses indicate that many children are quite capable of making connections between the politics and economics of war, and other socio-political issues such as the fire-fighters' strike. The quote above gives a clear answer to the question: should children accept a passive socio-political role at times of war? For the boy above, the answer (to use his favoured capitalisation) is NO.

Responding to First Edition: the Glasgow children and news survey

There is little space here to give detailed information about the survey of schoolchildren in Glasgow that our children and news research team has been conducting as a follow-up to our *First Edition* contacts.[13] However, to conclude this account of our work-in-progress on children's representation in the media, with particular reference to war coverage, I want to give some preliminary results from a survey and interviews conducted by Karin Wahl-Jorgensen and myself with primary schoolchildren in Glasgow in June 2003, a follow-up to a similar survey carried out by myself and Cindy Carter in June 2002, with children in the same schools (one of which included the children who had written regularly to *First Edition*). In 2002, the children's concerns were with the war in Afghanistan. In 2003, concern had shifted to the Iraqi war, but there were many common concerns from one year to the next – and a sophisticated understanding of the political and ideological links between the two wars, some of which has to be attributed to the children's relationship with *First Edition* – their regular viewing of it, and their regular letters to it.

On both occasions, children answered a detailed questionnaire and took part in focus groups. For the purposes of this brief essay, I have looked at the answers to just one of the questions in the 2003 questionnaire: 'How are children shown in adult news? Can you give an example you've seen recently?' This question sought to establish what children thought about the ways in which their contemporaries were represented in the media and whether they, too, noticed elements of 'passivity', 'emotionalism' and general victimhood. Many children – 25 out of 98 responses (25.5 per cent) – could not answer this question. They did not know what it meant, or did not know what to say; this rather puzzling inability will be discussed in more detail in future writing about our methodology. The remaining three quarters had no difficulties. All their answers were listed and coded, and the biggest proportion (20 per cent) were mentions of children being in danger in their own society: rape, murder, kidnap. This was also the case in our 2002 research, and reinforces other findings in studies on children and violence which indicate that children are much more distressed by 'real' violence, in recognisable settings than they are with either remote violence (such as foreign war) or fantasy violence.[14] Some specifically mentioned the Soham case, already nearly a year old – one child gave a precise list: 'Jessica and Holly; Milly; Sara Pain' (sic). 9 children – just over 9 per cent – mentioned the Iraqi war specifically and a further 6 – just over 6 per cent – mentioned the other side of the coin of childhood innocence: 'hooligans'; 'vandals'; 'thugs'. 4 mentioned children who were homeless or ill; three mentioned 'foreign children being ill' – one, optimistically, mentioned a positive view of 'foreign children', saying they were shown 'working and playing'. Altogether around 50 per cent of all responses talked about children being featured in a negative context, either as victims or as 'hooligans'. Leaving aside the 25 per cent who gave no response, only a quarter of the responses were positive – mentioning school stories, such as exam results; stories about Harry Potter and David Beckham and children making 'spectacular achievements'. Some were unspecific such as children being shown 'in pictures' or 'being interviewed'.

These answers relied on free recall – 'give an example you can remember' – and it is a feature of free recall that people will mention the most salient items in memory, with either very recent, or very strongly emotional or personally-meaningful events being prioritised. The proportions in these answers do not necessarily reflect the actual distribution of these stories in the news (although my small content analysis does, in fact, reveal a preponderance of victim-based stories about children). The emphasis given in these answers to stories about children like themselves being at risk, I suggest, is also a reflection of their anxieties about their own and their friends' safety. Such anxieties were also reflected in the focus group discussions – and are certainly there in the letters to *First Edition*. Such anxieties were expressed quite rationally and articulately; this further underlines the necessity of children themselves being considered by news-producers as competent to comment and participate in news stories about child-victims.

Scary news: children's responses to news of war

Cynthia Carter

How do children and young people deal with traumatic news events? And how do such events shape children's perceptions of themselves in an increasingly interconnected world? This article challenges the assumption that young people are unable to understand or cope with traumatic news. While children admitted they were frightened about the war in Iraq, what seemed to frighten some the most was that no one was listening to what they had to say about the decision to go to war. Many feel that adults need to accept that children and young people have certain rights and opinions that ought to be taken into account in important public debates.

It's like a disaster movie, except that it's real (Dorian, 11, Glasgow, *First Edition* online, September 12 2001).

Sometimes the news makes me feel ill, at how people have died etc. The news web site goes into so much detail (it makes you want to cry), it's all real stuff, is not the movies (Ro, 12, Cumbria, CBBC *Newsround* online, 17 October 2002).

A now widespread misconception is that children naturally find the news to be boring unless it is about pop stars, sports or animals. Sometimes, though, there are events that occur, such as the attacks on the World Trade Centre and Pentagon on 11 September 2001, that provide a clear demonstration that many children are not only aware of and interested in what is going on in the world, but also that they often have a sophisticated understanding of the top stories covered in adult news. One of the comments quoted above came from a letter written to an online children's news site in response to the 11 September attacks on the US (these and other comments were posted on UK Channel Four Television's *First Edition* website and Children's BBC (CBBC) *Newsround* children's news website shortly afterwards). There was a truly remarkable response from British children generated by these events – for instance, a jump from 200 to 2,000 letters and e-mails in the week immediately after to *Newsround* producers, and an outpouring of concerned and agonised messages on the worldwide web. The first comment, from Dorian, echoes many adult comments about the apparently fictional nature of the visual coverage of the attacks. However, this child, like the other children who wrote to children's news producers, was in no doubt that what she was seeing was real. Thousands of children do not write to or e-mail television broadcasters and children's news websites in response to disaster movies. The other quotation above was written by a child responding to the CBBC *Newsround* story in October 2002 that invited children to tell them if the news sometimes upsets them.

In this essay, I want to address what I believe to be several important and inter-related debates around children and citizenship, the now seriously deteriorating provision of children's broadcast and online news resources, and children's online responses to traumatic news events. Research undertaken in each of these areas has largely neglected to make what I think are extremely important connections between the following three areas. Firstly, the recent introduction of citizenship studies in UK schools and the establishment of organisations like the *Institute for Citizenship* point to increasingly serious political concerns around the future of citizen participation in democratic decision-making in society. Secondly, many journalists and news media scholars worry what a diminishing provision of meaningful and critical children's news in all of its forms (print, broadcast and internet) may mean for children's desire to become informed citizens who will one day take seriously their responsibilities for public decision making. Thirdly, my preliminary analysis of children's use of chat rooms and message boards clearly shows that some children are not at all reluctant to talk about significant issues in the news.[1] It is this largely untapped potential for public sphere debate amongst children that I think warrants a closer look, because it may hold one of the keys for understanding how best to engage children in the world around them, thereby making concrete current political and educational aims to encourage in them active citizenship. The broad-based primary and secondary education around citizenship in the UK, whilst essentially worthy, is, in my view, rather abstract where issues around global citizenship are concerned, but also too focused on local and personal issues to engage children with some of the most pressing issues that will face them as adults in an increasingly globalised world.

What I have found particularly interesting in my research is that children on the *Newsround* message boards are continuing to exchange passionate arguments about the decision to go to war in Iraq and whether or not now is the time to hand back control of the country to Iraqis. Although both the children's and adults' news media no longer spend much time discussing the causes of the war in Iraq, it is interesting to follow the almost daily conversations amongst a group of children who think this issue is still relevant. In this essay, I want to make an initial attempt to link these three general areas of public and academic interest and concern. My central argument is that children only find the news to be frightening (or boring) when they feel they are not being taken seriously and that their opinions and ideas don't count for anything. When programmes like *First Edition* reach children and are able to address them as citizens in the making, children then tend to feel much more empowered and interested in the world around them. When they get the message that the adult world thinks they are incapable of understanding serious issues, and when there are fewer children's news outlets producing the news for child audiences, it is hardly surprising that young people would find news and politics to be unintelligible, frightening, boring or, indeed, a great waste of their time.

In order to begin the task of making these connections, what I do here, in a necessarily rather limited way, is explore children's online responses to news about war and conflict – specifically, the 11 September 2001 attacks on the US, and the spring 2003 war in Iraq and its aftermath. I have chosen these types of events rather than any others precisely because they throw into sharpest relief the issues with which children often most passionately engage. For me, this provides a clear example of the potential that lies in providing a wider array of children's news resources (print, broadcast and online). Such a provision would enable children not only to better understand the news more generally, but also to voice their opinions about how the news is put together and the events it covers, and to have a critical awareness of the political assumptions underpinning current children's and adult's new provision in the UK.

Due to limitations of space, I am only able to draw upon the CBBC website for *Newsround* and from Channel 4 Television's website for the now defunct children's news programme, *First Edition*. My choice of these two websites is partly to do with the fact that they are readily available and offer children easy access to child friendly explanations of up to date news stories, and spaces in which to interact with other children I have structured this essay as follows. Firstly, I begin by briefly examining UK national government educational policy on citizenship studies and the promotion of what they call the 'active citizen'. I do so in order to consider both the strengths and limitations of a strategy that they hope will encourage children to 'think critically about their role in society and their potential as agents of change'. [2] In a second section, I provide a short summary of the current state of the UK's children's news provision. I will look at certain print, broadcast and online resources to show that while there is really very little available that is produced by and/or for children (particularly true with regard to the public service media), there remains a high interest amongst children in important news events, particularly amongst those who are the most 'media literate'. I also offer a few comments from a research project with which I am involved that has been examining children's responses to traumatic news events because it provides some concrete support for my assertion.[3] In a third and final section, I engage with a range of children's responses to news about war and conflict. Most of these I have gathered from online resources (CBBC *Newsround* and C4's *First Edition*), although I also rely on full letters written by children to *First Edition* producers, some of which were posted online on the *First Edition* website.

Active citizenship

One of the key political buzzwords in the UK today is that of citizenship.[4] For quite some time, political leaders have noted that participation in elections, local and national, has been steadily falling. The 2001 General Election had the lowest voter turnout since 1918 – fewer than 60 per cent of those eligible to vote in 2001 actually cast their ballot. Political leaders decided that this situation was a result of voter disaffection, and sought to address, in earnest, voter disillusionment with political institutions. The Institute for Citizenship, an independent charitable trust established in 1992 by former Speaker of the House of Commons, the Rt Hon. Bernard Weatherill MP, has produced what they refer to as 'citizenship education resources' for teachers and students.[5] One example is the 'Democracy through Citizenship' project funded for three years by the Joseph Rowntree Foundation, which has developed a National Curriculum Key Stage 3 unit called 'Introduction to Citizenship'. In this unit, children learn about the concepts of community and individual rights and responsibilities. Community is defined primarily as a local concept (home, school, town/city). Similarly, the UK government Department for Education and Skills (DfES) has developed guidelines and schemes for teaching about citizenship in primary and secondary schools. Its Citizenship site offers information for teachers, pupils and parents about citizenship study, outlining what they believe to be the main issues, and how to define what citizenship means.[6] Firstly, it is about 'social and moral responsibility', where the emphasis is on building pupils' 'self confidence and socially and morally responsible behaviour both in and beyond the classroom'. Secondly, citizenship entails 'community involvement'. Children are encouraged to become involved in the activities of people in their community and to learn 'through community involvement and service to the community'. Finally, a good citizen is described as one who is 'politically literate'. What this means is that children are being encouraged to learn about 'the institutions, problems and practices of our democracy and how to make themselves effective in the life of the nation, locally, regionally and nationally through skills and values as well as knowledge – a concept wider than political knowledge alone'.[7]

What is immediately apparent from both of these examples of attempts to deal with voter apathy and disillusionment in political institutions is an emphasis on the local – upon building up a sense of informed and active citizenship at the level of the most immediate community in which children live. Whilst this is a laudable aim, what is marginalised is discussion about children's place and importance within national and international communities of people. Whilst one can build from the local, it seems to me that this overemphasis on the local, right up to the age of 16, does not adequately address the need for children to feel connected across a range of communities.

In a world that is increasingly interconnected socially, economically, politically and technologically, constructing a sense of community and shared responsibility necessarily must go beyond the local, so that children have the resources to better engage with globalised political issues. One key way in which children can do this most easily is through their engagement with the news, where they can find out about events that are happening close to their homes, within the rest of the country, and around the world. Being news literate should neither be taken for granted nor dismissed as unimportant, particularly where children are concerned. Children find out about what is happening outside their local environment not only by talking to their peers, teachers and parents, but also through what they can glean from the news media. If we are not prepared to teach them how to be critical news consumers, then how can we expect them to form opinions with which they question and at times challenge those who have most political power in society? When a child is given a chance to understand what is in the media and why, how it is produced, who produces it, and in whose interests, and who is given greatest space to speak, then what happens is that that child begins forming their own views. This, in turn, is likely to make them feel much more empowered and thus connected to the world around them – if they are being listened to and taken seriously, then they will speak. It is at this point that they become active citizens – when they feel able to exercise the freedom of speech that is supposedly the right of all in liberal democratic society. Of course, important in this regard is the provision of children's news since this is where there is potential for children to engage with the news – where the news is covered in a way that is accessible, interesting and relevant to their lives. In the next section of this essay, I briefly look at the main forms of children's news provision available in the UK, in order to outline what is available and to argue that much more needs to be done to ensure that children are addressed as a particular type of news audience – as citizens in the making.

UK children's news provision – traditional and online

With the demise of Channel 4 Television's weekly 15-minute children's news programme, *First Edition*, the UK television market has been left with no provision for serious, sustained children's broadcast journalism. While *Newsround* does cover many important news topics on its daily weekday 5-minute newscast at 5.25 (and daily 3-minute bulletins on at 1.00 pm on weekdays), it is primarily concerned with stories about celebrities, sports, interesting facts, and UK regional stories related to children. The *Newsround* website, however, covers a broader range of issues, including more serious topics – recently there have been stories of Nigerian children being abducted and sold into slavery, gun control, the UN vote on the US/UK proposal for Iraq, the need for better information about AIDS in the developing world, and the trial of Ian Huntley for the murders of Holly Wells and Jessica Chapman.

In this section, I will outline some of the features of children's news provision in the UK, including the now defunct *First Edition*. In all four cases, each provider has had a web presence of some description, with only *Newsround* having interactive and web chat capabilities. While print or broadcast children's news in the UK assumes that its audience is primarily a national one, what makes online news provision is unique is the fact that any child in the world with access to the Internet can log on. This point is most obvious when looking at web chat on *Newsround*, where web chat visitors include children from around the world. These UK based websites have helped to create spaces for international dialogue, particularly on the message board entitled 'what's in the news', where children engage with topics currently in the news and discuss their views with other children.

The Newspaper

The Newspaper is a commercially-based national tabloid print and online newspaper for eight- to thirteen- year-olds, produced by adult journalists and teachers twice a term (six times per year). It was developed as an educational tool for teachers to use with children in the final years of primary school and the early years of secondary school. With each issue, fifty free copies are mailed directly to schools across the UK. If a school needs more than fifty copies, then it must pay an annual subscription, with ten additional copies six times per year costing £18 and 150 extra copies costing £267. *The Newspaper* relies almost entirely on advertising revenue for its income. Various companies advertise in both the print and online versions and sometimes pay the newspaper to run competitions which children are encouraged to enter. Advertisers in the October 2003 issue of the online publication were Busch Gardens, Sea World, Discovery Cove – all in the US – Dance UK Playstation game, and a public service advertisement linking *The Newspaper* with the A4ME website which has information resources for sufferers of ME.[8]

The online version of *The Newspaper* is updated every four weeks. Whilst it is less detailed than the print version, it is accessible on the Internet free of charge. The online version includes sections on home and world news, leisure, the environment, sport, science and technology, and the opportunity to email the editor with feedback on *The Newspaper*'s stories.

In addition to its news content, *The Newspaper* has also produced, online, worksheets which teachers can use in lessons around a range of issues, utilising *The Newspaper* as a non-fiction resource. Parents are also targeted by the website, being told that *The Newspaper* can be used to address issues around citizenship and social responsibility, which are new features of the National Curriculum. Parents are encouraged to get their children to e-mail the editor as a way of developing their citizenship skills.

Children's Express

The original idea came from the USA, where Bob Clampitt, who is a former Wall Street lawyer and business entrepreneur, launched a newspaper of the same name in 1975. According to the UK *Children's Express* (*CE*) website (www.childrens-express.org/):

> Clampitt believed passionately that what children think and say does matter ... What began as a publication 'by children for children' soon evolved into a news service that provided columns, articles, radio and TV programmes across the United States.

Unfortunately, US *CE* ceased publication on 30 June 2001 due to insufficient funding for its operations. Bureaux affected were New York, Washington DC, Marquette, Michigan and a bureau in Tokyo, Japan. UK *CE* was not affected by these closures since it is an independent UK charity.

In 1994, four teenagers from New York came to Britain to train thirty UK children to become *CE* journalists. UK *CE* opened on 25 May 1995, originally with only one office – in London. More than seventy children had been recruited from the community to work on the paper, with two thirds coming from ethnic minorities. Channel 4 newsreader, Jon Snow, who later went on to anchor the Channel 4 Television children's news programme, *First Edition,* helped to launch the paper. *CE* currently has bureaux in London, Birmingham, Sheffield, Newcastle, Belfast and Plymouth, and plans to possibly open one in Cardiff. The motto prominently displayed on *CE*'s website is 'Written by children for everyone'. What they mean by that is that their stories are written by children from their points of view, but the main aim of their work is to get these stories taken up by adult news providers to help fund *CE* activities and to more widely circulate children's views in society. The UK website was launched in 1998, and was re-launched in 2002 with easier web navigation. Guardian Online journalists and web designers volunteered to help *CE* journalists in this task.

In September 2002, *CE* launched new online materials that could be used in classroom citizenship lessons, entitled *Citizen's Express*. Partly funded by the UK

Department for Education and Skills as well as by Learnthings and the Peabody Trust, the aim of this website is to provide online stories and other resources that teachers can use to enhance discussion about topical issues in the classroom and in assemblies. CE currently has almost 700 stories in their online archive from 1994 to the present. They have also developed Key Stage 3 and 4 Citizenship syllabi – the Key Stage 4 syllabus consists of the following topics: teenage pregnancy; crime; family; racism; homelessness; and, poverty. The developers of this syllabus claim that it is meant to be used in conjunction with the *Children's Express* story library, available online, to be used as a classroom resource. While this is certainly a step in the right direction, again, it does little to teach children not involved on the newspaper about news literacy – a skill that *CE* journalists themselves clearly have. They state that their involvement in writing stories for *CE* has helped them to become 'better-informed, more self-assured citizens' who through their work have learned to 'think critically, to work together and, crucially, to express themselves with confidence.'[9]

Children's BBC (CBBC) Newsround

The very first transmission of BBC television's children's news programme, *Newsround*, took place on 4 April 1972. There were only three journalists working on stories for the programme, at desks in a corner of BBC News' foreign newsroom. It was the idea of the then deputy head of children's programmes, Edward Barnes, who was motivated partly by an interest in developing news for children (aged 8-14) and partly by the need to fill the time gaps that resulted from airing programmes of different durations. The first series, anchored by former BBC Bristol journalist John Craven, was initially aired on Tuesday and Wednesday each week for a total duration of six weeks. Because the programme was very successful in terms of attracting a sufficiently large audience, it was brought back in September 1972 for a six-month run, aired on Wednesdays and Thursdays. By 1974, it was firmly established as a regular prime time feature of BBC television. When it returned after the summer break on 9 September, the BBC had increased the frequency of its transmission to four days a week (from Monday to Thursday). By 1975, *Newsround* was regularly attracting an audience of 5.5 million children. A *Radio Times* article published on 6 September 1975 noted that 55 per cent of all 5-7 year olds regularly tuned in to the programme. The same article quoted Alan Protheroe, then deputy editor of BBC TV News, who insisted: 'What delighted us was the way it quickly became clear they were going to carry real news.'

What is interesting to note in terms of the child audience of the time is the extent to which children were becoming regular news consumers because of the development of *Newsround*. The importance of increasing the provision of children's news programming was clear to one journalist at the *Evening Standard* newspaper who wrote: 'Those who watch are more likely to become VSO volunteers than hooligans.' When *Newsround* returned after the summer break in 1979, for the first time it stayed on year round instead of breaking for the summer holidays.

In 1983, *Newsround* launched its mock election, run alongside the General Election, which allowed children to vote for local (student) candidates in schools. In its first year, hundreds of thousands of children voted and have continued to vote at every General Election since. In 1985, *Newsround* was given high praise by *Times* journalist Mark Lawson who declared, '*Newsround* is one of the glorious success stories of British television. The originally unwanted little brother got the format right first time and maintains its level of excellence. A ten minute mix of global disaster and dancing dolphins.'

After being the main anchor for fifteen years, John Craven was still a favourite with children in 1987. In that year, a BBC poll indicated that 96 per cent of children aged ten to fifteen thought John was a good presenter. It was not until 1988 that *Newsround* began to use child reporters. The response from children was overwhelming and led *Newsround* producers to develop the *Newsround* Newshound club (later renamed the Press Pack), which at one point had as many as 120,000 members. At the end of the 1980s, on 22 June 1989, John Craven left *Newsround* to present the BBC programme, *Countryfile*.

Over the course of the 1990s, *Newsround* went through substantial changes – including nine presenters, almost all of whom were very young adult presenters at the beginning of their career, five sets and four theme tunes. In 2001, *Newsround* launched both its website and seven new bulletins on the CBBC digital television channel. The website clearly offers more scope for children to engage with a wider array of issues in the news, and is one of the few truly interactive sites for children's news. One disappointing development, however, has been the axing of the weekly Sunday evening news roundup for children, *Newsround 24*, which was formerly aired on BBC News 24.

Channel Four Television – First Edition and Citizen Power

First Edition was a weekly, fifteen-minute children's news programme broadcast in the mid-morning, anchored by Channel 4 News journalist Jon Snow. It was broadcast for use in schools from 1997-2002. The programme was developed by Channel 4 Television for eight- to fourteen- year-old children as part of Channel 4's '4Learning' educational provision. The programme aired each week on Tuesday morning, and was repeated at the same time on Thursday during most of the school year (from mid September to April). Its main aim was to encourage children to engage with current events and to become active and critical news audiences. Unlike more recent children's news initiatives like *Citizen's Express, The Newspaper* and *Citizen Power*, the programme's producers did not see it as part of their job to develop worksheets or lesson plans for teachers to use in conjunction with the programme.

The adult journalistic team put most of the journalism on the television programme together, with some feedback input from children in different parts of the country. Typically, only three news stories were covered in a programme, to allow *First Edition* journalists to provide sufficient depth and explanation so that children would best be able to understand what were often very complex and confusing stories – most of which were also being covered in adult news at the same time. A regular feature of the weekly programme was the inclusion of a different child reporter who was responsible for presenting a news story or interviewing an invited guest to supplement the story.

The *First Edition* website (recently deleted) included an archive of the weekly stories featured in the television programme, postings from feedback letters on various topics posted to programme producers, and background information on politics and current issues in the news. The site also featured a space that included children's feedback to *First Edition* producers, but there was no interactive message board that could be used for children to discuss the news with each other.

By the end of November 2002, *First Edition* had ceased production. In personal interviews with the programme's producer, Lea Sellars, and the news anchor, Jon Snow, both indicated that a main reason behind the show's cancellation was its short shelf life as a commercial product.[10] With increased competition in the children's programming sector and a stated desire to come up with a current affairs programme that could be sold to wider (foreign) markets over a longer period of time, Channel 4 executives decided to replace *First Edition* with a monthly magazine series called *Citizen Power*. The programme is broadcast during the school day on the first Tuesday of each month and repeated on the remaining Tuesdays. Rather than focus on current news issues which required the rapid development of a news agenda, story gathering and reporting, *Citizen Power* looks more broadly at current issues that they think are of interest to children (issues such as law making, voting, and biodiversity have been covered to date). *Citizen Power* focuses on local, national and global issues that can be used by teachers in delivering the National Curriculum on a wide range of citizenship issues. It is put together by adult journalists who work for Independent Television News (ITN) and some child reporters. Children are encouraged to use the website to find out what's coming up each month, to send their comments to the programme, and join in the monthly polls asking them for their views on the issues raised in the programmes.

While on the surface it would appear that the above demonstrates that there is a fairly wide array of children's news resources in the UK, I would argue that this is not the case, and that the UK provision of current news issues for child audiences is now terribly weak. Most of these news enterprises have constructed their online sites around stories that can be used to deliver the UK government's citizenship curriculum. There is money to be made in the development of teachers' worksheets, teaching packs and in taking out subscriptions to newspapers that can be used to teach about citizenship.

Nowhere is British children's news more deficient than in the area of up to date daily and weekly serious news stories – particularly around war and conflict, where there is little news specifically tailored for child audiences. It strikes me as rather odd that such issues, ones that children themselves identify as being of vital importance to them in their development as critically aware and active global citizens, are often those which are less well addressed in children's news. In the next section of this essay, I look specifically at children's responses to these issues through their web chat on the CBBC *Newsround* website – from quotations in news stories as well as feedback to the 'what's in the news' message board. I do so to demonstrate the extent to which children are aware of the issues, show great desire to be better informed, and also want to have their views taken seriously by the rest of society. Children's news that primarily reports about animals, sports and pop stars and is presented by bright, sparky young people who are not necessarily journalists, assumes that these issues are just about the only ones that interest children. I asked children whom I interviewed if this was true. Their resounding response was that what they really wanted was to be taken seriously. To do that, children's news would have to cover important, up to the minute issues and use experienced journalists to report them (particularly well liked was Jon Snow on *First Edition*). Some also suggested that news stories covered by child reporters should become a regular feature of adult news. This, they claimed, would ensure that adults were regularly made aware of children's points of view and demonstrate that adults regarded their views as important contributions to public sphere debates. Some of these responses are addressed in the next section of this essay, where I directly explore children's responses to news about war and conflict.

Children's responses to the war and conflict

Few researchers have examined how children talk about traumatic news events and how they might shape children's perceptions of themselves in an increasingly globalised world.[11] In this section, I examine how children have responded online to news about the war in Iraq and its aftermath. Because of the limited space I have to provide illustrations, I am only able to focus on one example. At the time of writing, the war in Iraq had been officially over for more than six months (having been declared so by George Bush in early May 2003). However, the everyday reality of life in Iraq is that attacks on Iraqi citizens, and soldiers of the US/UK coalition continue with seemingly no let up.

I focus here on how children who engage with the news through children's news websites appear to be using the web as a one of many strategies for understanding these ongoing news events, how they see their own and other children's place in the world, and how the news may shape their thoughts on their citizenship as children.[12] Preliminary research that I have undertaken with colleagues examining children's relationship to the news suggests that, while children ask to have their views taken seriously, they also conclude that adults are largely unaware of and uninterested in what children have to say about the political significance of such events. The same is true in comments that I have read on the CBBC *Newsround* website. What I have found from reading various opinions around children and traumatic news is that a central focus is how adults can protect children. When protection is not possible, the advice is always that adults have to find ways to deal with children's fears and to shield them from the real horrors of such events.[13] Here, the assumption is that children are unable to understand and unable to cope with traumatic news and that therefore all one can do as a parent, teacher or other significant adult in a child's life is to turn their reactions into an individualised response that can be handled through psychological counselling.[14]

Such views about how children relate to traumatic news events need to be re-thought so that we can better engage with the ways in which children say they experience such events. Much of the current research on this issue is informed by social psychology. Researchers tend to assume that children, particularly pre-adolescent children, are unable to understand or cope with traumatic news events; this is an argument that has permeated civil society to such an extent that it is now more or less accepted without question as the only appropriate way to address children's responses to traumatic news.[15] Here, it is seen to be the responsibility of parents to ask their children if they have any questions and to provide reassurance that the child is personally safe. The parental role is not to explain, analyse or critique the reporting of a traumatic event in the news, but to monitor their child's emotional responses and to look out for psychological and physiological symptoms that that child may be suffering. The central concern, it seems, is to mitigate any negative effect traumatic news may have on children. In my view, this widely accepted approach underestimates children's abilities to understand, critique and cope with frightening news. Looking at the ways in which CBBC news online reported the war in Iraq, for example, supports a position that children want and need to know about such events and to have their views heard and taken seriously by adults. Said fifteen-year-old Becca from Weybridge on *CBBC*'s online site on 25 March 2003:

> If people would listen to children properly as if what we had to say was important (which it is) they would see the easiest way to sort things out. We, as children, see things simpler, without thinking about pride, shame or POLITICS. War is something adults do for pride and politics, they can't admit they are wrong.

While children admitted in online news sites that they were frightened about the war in Iraq, what seemed to frighten some the most was that no one was listening to them. Children repeatedly tell adults that they want to be accepted as citizens with certain opinions and rights. After all, that is only fair. They have to live with the consequences of the actions of decisions taken by adults yet have little chance to influence these decisions This point was made most clearly by ten-year-old Cara-Leigh from Arlesey who said:

> I am very scared about the war with Iraq, because President Bush and Tony Blair are not giving our selves, 'children' a chance to speak about it, because it may change our lives (*CBBC online* 25 March 2003).

In early March 2003, hundreds of school pupils across the UK walked out of school to join anti-war marches. Five hundred or so made their way to the Prime Minister's residence at 10 Downing Street and held a sit-in at the gates to the street, blocking it. Children around the world joined peace marches when and where they could. Ally, sixteen, from Manchester, was very pleased that the march she went on included many children who were there with family or friends. On this fact, Ally remarked,

> I went down to London for the march against the war in Iraq. I think the amount of CHILDREN who did really shows what the adults of tomorrow will be like. Better.

Ally's view of children's willingness to become informed about the war in Iraq and to join peace marches where their presence and voices would count for something echoes that of many other children on CBBC *Newround* online. While of course some children supported the war, most did not, and they were not afraid to say that war did not solve anything regardless of the situation (even whilst many agreed that Saddam Hussein was an evil dictator). A prevailing view amongst many of the children is that children already know and appreciate the fact that war kills and does far more damage than it helps in any situation.

This point is echoed by another girl, Nicole, who responded to a CBBC news item that reported that twenty-six special episodes of *Sesame Street*, entitled *Sesame Stories*, have been made in an effort to promote peace in the Middle East. This was to be achieved in the programme through the use of Israeli and Arab Muppets who form friendships, thus creating role models for mutual understanding, respect and cross cultural co-operation. An EU representative noted the importance of promoting peace through reaching child audiences, noting that 'Working with children today will help build peace tomorrow' (CBBC *Newsround*, 21 October 2002). However, Nicole is sceptical about the immediate worth of Sesame stories aimed at children, because in her view it is adults who need to listen to such messages much more than children. Claims Nicole:

i think this might be a good idea, but only to children, who after all want peace anyway dont they? they dont need a special edition to sesame street to tell them that, altho twill be entertaining for them. it's the adults who need to make peace, children dont have the power to start peace treaties, so i think the show is aimed at the wrong audience.

nicole xx **Reply** (CBBC online 21 October 2003).

By far the most sustained debate recently occurred between children who were broadly supportive of the effort to rid Iraq of Saddam Hussein and those who were not only critical of the war, but also of the governments in both the US and UK. Responding to a message asking if there was anyone who actually supported the war (and if they did, they were mad), an exchange occurred over the space of a few days, two of which are included here.

re: jst out of a matter of interest
Smart – 11th post – 14 Sep 2003 15:21

Ask your self this; Would the people of Iraq have suffered more if they had continued to live under Saddam's rein? Living in a world where you can not voice your opinion freely and if anything is said against the govenment having a severe punishment (often disgusting forms of torture like the electric chair). Is this really a world in which the people of Iraq anted to keep on living in? Yes-innocent people died but on the scale of things if action had not been taken now more people would have died under HIS terrible rein. War is not the solution to anything but people as cruel and as harsh as him refuse to be reasoned with and war perhaps is the only answer … Luv Smart Gal

Later on that day, 'MuLlet' responded to 'Smart Gal' and others who were writing in to respond to the chat thread, to challenge the view that war in Iraq was probably inevitable. In MuLlet's contribution to this subject, she/he argued that the United States government seemed willing to sacrifice thousands of innocent lives in order to catch just two men, Saddam Hussein and Osama bin Laden.

re: jst out of a matter of interest
~*.ˌˏ.·´¨`»MuLleT«´¨`·.ˌˏ.*~_ – 1916th post – 14 Sep 2003 18:16

Ahem! In case u didnt no the USA uses the electric chair tho i do agree its horrible. And no war is good! How cud u say it is? Numbers don't matter when it's people getting killed and i think NO1 deserves death. Also u cant say thers no irony that bush killed lodza innocent ppl jst 2 get 2 men (ben laden and saddam)and did he even catch them? nooooo. Id hav thought bush would no btr bout killin innocent ppl after 9/11 but apparently hes 2 narrowminded. And now hes talking about the 'rebuildin' of iraq which seems to consist of killing more ppl and also ,it seems, splittin iraq up between a few countries (tho they seem 2 hav conveniantly not mentioned this on english tv) I beleive 4 a country 2 really be freed it has to come from inside or else they wil hav 2 liv in debt to another country which is not bein free.

In March 2003, many British children took part in anti-war demonstrations around the country. It was noted at the time that these events were well organised, in part because children used the Internet and mobile phone texting to make other children aware of the issues and where to go to demonstrate.

Noreen, sixteen, who lives in Pakistan, responded to the question *Newsround* asked its web audience as to whether or not they marched against the war in March 2003 by saying that:

> I didn't march because it can get very violent here, but if I could I would have. They should listen to what wee have to say. Bush has no excuse to kill millions of innocent people to get Saddam out of the way and even if there was a war what good will come out of it? Bush should see what the rest of the world has to say. Not the leader, PM or presidents, but what the public has to say. Let us all say NO to war.

Even though, officially, the war in Iraq has been over some time now, a steady stream of children continue to discuss this topic on the *Newsround* website – both those in favour of the action and those who remain opposed to it. Some children appear to be concerned about the role of the US and UK governments in what they see as a largely politically (US/UK economic self interest – cheap oil) rather than morally motivated mission, as both leaders tried to declare before, during and after the war. Clearly, amongst many UK children writing to *Newsround*'s 'What's in the News?' message board, as well as children in other parts of the world (including the USA, Pakistan, Canada, and Germany), many (although not all) did not accept the reasons given by leaders in the US and UK.

Conclusions

News about the war and current conflict in Iraq continues to engage the imaginations of many children and this is clearly being expressed online on message boards, despite the fact that this story is not usually at the top of the daily news agenda in adult news, and even less so in children's news. Many children cut their political news teeth on the tragic events of 11 September 2001, and the wars in Afghanistan and Iraq. As a result, some have made great efforts to become more aware, engaged and active citizens. One child that I spoke to in Glasgow only nine months after 11 September noted how important this event and the subsequent war in Afghanistan are for his generation, suggesting that they might, in the end, be as significant as World War II to his grandparents' generation or Vietnam to his parents'. In his view, it is important for children's news to cover these events in a way that was understandable (but not patronising) and thus reassuring for child audiences, without pulling punches and hiding frightening facts from them. This view is similar to that of twelve-year-old Leigh from Grantham who responded to *Newsround* online's question to children just after the first anniversary of 11 September 2001, asking them if stories in the news scare them. Leigh said,

> I think news does scare children. When I heard about September 11th, I was scared in case they were going to bomb us, but when I heard Newsround it was less frightening and helps me understand this more, like bombing.

On the first anniversary of the attacks on the US, the following two children had this to say on the *Newround* website about its effect on their awareness around world events and their individual responsibility to stay informed:

> It really made me realise how bad life is for some people and it's made me pay more attention to what's going on in the world. It was really, really terrible! Susan, 13, Swindon (*Newsround* online 13 September 2002)

> It's made me watch the news more and be aware of what's happening in the world. Frankie, 13, London (*Newsround* online, 13 September 2002).

What we now desperately need are children's news media that such politically aware and active young global citizens deserve to ensure that they continue to feel so engaged and empowered for the rest of their political lives – and which will encourage other children to join them.

References

Buckingham, D. (1993), *Children Talking Television: The Making of Television Literacy*, Falmer, London.

Buckingham, D. (1996), *Moving Images: Understanding Children's Emotional Responses to Television*, Manchester and New York: Manchester University Press.

Buckingham, D. (2000), *The Making of Citizens: Young People, News and Politics*, London: Routledge.

Cantor, J. (2001), 'The Media and Children's Fears, Anxieties, and Perceptions of Danger', in Singer, Dorothy G., and Singer, Jerome L. (Eds), *Handbook of Children and the Media*, Sage, Thousand Oaks, pp207-22.

Carter, C. (2002), 'Children, news and the public sphere', International Communication Association annual conference, *Reconciliation through Communication*, Feminist Scholarship Division Panel, International Communication Association, Seoul, Korea, 15-19 July.

Carter, C., Messenger Davies, M., and Allan, S. (2003), 'Children's News Talk', International Communication Association annual conference *Communication in Borderlands*, Mass Communication Division Panel, San Diego, USA, 23-27 May.

Carter, C., Messenger Davies, M., Allan, S., and Wahl-Jorgensen, K. (2002), 'Children, news and September 11: A case study of Scottish children's responses', *After September 11: TV News and Transnational Audiences* seminar, Stanhope Centre for Communications Policy Research, London, England, 9-11 September.

Carter, C., Messenger Davies, M, Allan, S. and Wahl-Jorgensen, K. (2002), 'Coping with September 11: Children's responses to television news', International Communication Association annual conference, *Reconciliation through Communication*, Popular Communication Division Panel, Seoul, Korea, 15-19 July.

CBBC Newsround (2003), 'Children "should improve web use"', (accessed 17 October 2003).

Citizen Power (2003), (accessed 17 October 2003).

Crick, B. (2000), *Essays on Citizenship*, Continuum, London.

Davies, M. M. (2001), '*Dear BBC': Children, television storytelling and the public sphere*, Cambridge University Press, Cambridge.

Department for Education and Skills (DfES), (2003), .

Donnerstein, Edward (2002), 'The Internet', in Strasburger, Victor C. and Wilson, Barbara J. *Children, Adolescents, and the Media*, Sage, Thousand Oaks, pp301-21.

Furlong, Andy and Cartmel, Fred (1997), 'Politics and Participation', *Young People and Social Change: Individualization and Risk in Late Modernity*, Open University Press, Buckingham and Philadelphia, pp96-108.

Groebel, J. (2001), Media Violence in Cross-Cultural Perspective: A Global Study on Children's Media Behaviour and Some Educational Implications', in Singer, Dorothy G., and Singer, Jerome L. (eds), *Handbook of Children and the Media*, Sage, Thousand Oaks, pp255-68.

Institute for Citizenship (2003), (accessed 17 October 2003).

Lemish, D. (1998). 'What is News? A Cross-Cultural Examination of Kindergartners' Understanding of News', *Communication: European Journal of Communication Research*, 23, pp491-504.

Livingstone, S. (2002), *Young People and New Media*. London: Sage.

Montgomery, K.C. (2001), 'Digital Kids: The New On-Line Children's Consumer Culture', in Singer, Dorothy G., and Singer, Jerome L. (Eds), *Handbook of Children and the Media*, Sage, Thousand Oaks, pp635-50.

Paik, H. (2001), 'The History of Children's Use of Electronic Media', Singer, Dorothy G., and Jerome L. Singer (Eds), *Handbook of Children and the Media*, Sage, Thousand Oaks, pp7-28.

Tarpley, T. (2001), 'Children, the Internet, and Other New Technologies', in Singer, Dorothy G., and Jerome L. Singer (Eds), *Handbook of Children and the Media*, Sage, Thousand Oaks, pp547-56.

The Newspaper (2003), (accessed 17 October 2003).

Wartella, E. and N. Jennings (2001), 'Hazards and Possibilities of Commercial TV in the Schools', Singer, Dorothy G., and Jerome L. Singer (Eds), *Handbook of Children and the Media*, Sage, Thousand Oaks, pp557-70.

Notes

1. See also Donnerstein, 2002; Livingstone, 2002; Paik, 2001; Tarpley, 2001.
2. Institute for Citizenship, 2003.
3. Research undertaken with children aged 10-11 at Hillhead Primary School in Glasgow with colleagues Stuart Allan, School of Cultural Studies, University of the West of England, Bristol, and Cardiff School of Journalism, Media and Cultural Studies, Cardiff University colleagues Máire Messenger Davies and Karin Wahl-Jorgensen. Every week, Year 7 teacher Ms Marjorie Maclean's class watched *First Edition*, discussed it and then wrote letters to the programme's producers.
4. See Children's Express, 2003; Crick, 2000; Department of Education and Skills, 2003; Furlong and Cartmel, 1997).
5. See www.citizen.org.uk.education.html.
6. See www.dfes.gov.uk/citizenship.
7. See ibid (accessed 21 October 2003).
8. For a discussion about the difficulties associated with commercial media in schools, see Wartella and Jennings, 2001 and for a discussion about children's online consumer culture see Montgomery, 2001.
9. See www.childrens-express.org/teachers/index.htm (accessed 24 October 2003).
10. Personal interview on 3 February 2003.
11. Notable exceptions to this are found in the work of Buckingham 2000; Carter, 2002; Carter, Messenger Davies and Allan 2003; Carter, Messenger Davies, Allan and Wahl-Jorgensen, 2002; Davies 2001; Lemish 1998).
12. I have gathered similar data around the traumatic events of September 11 from various children's news websites as well as responses to the war in Afghanistan. However, I am unable in this short paper to present this data.
13. See Cantor, 2001; Groebel, 2001).
14. See, for example, American Academy of Child & Adolescent Psychiatry (2002) 'Children and the News', (accessed 10 July 2002); Center for Media Literacy (2002) 'Trauma on the News: Should Children Watch:' (accessed 14 February 2003). Unitarian Universalist Association, 'Helping Children in Response to Today's News', (2001) (accessed 16 October 2003).
15. This is particularly true in the US, where psychological counselling is widely accepted as a way of dealing with problems – by individualising children's responses to traumatic news.
16. CBBC *Newsround*, March 3 2003 (accessed 28 March 2003).

The Iraqi war and the web

Paul Rixon

The start of the Iraqi war heralded a new kind of information war. No longer was the public solely dependent on the traditional news media for information. With the spread of the world-wide web, at least in the industrialised nations, a new means by which to perceive and experience war had arrived. This article explores the different ways the web allowed users to actively shape their understanding of the Iraq war, whether by accessing websites, participating in online discussions, interacting with news sites, or exploring government and military sites. Does this diversity of information lead to the end of popular support for war or will the development of new media strategies by the military counter these developments?

As the US and British military swept into Iraq in 2003, so started what was arguably one of the first digital wars.[1] American commanders were able to follow and control, in real time, through their intranet, the various parts of the military machine in a way not previously thought possible outside of science fiction. With real time intelligence being collected by satellite, surveillance aircraft, predator aircraft and units on the ground, allied commanders were provided with a virtual simulation of the war within their command bunkers – this was network centric warfare. This was a war more akin to a computer game than any which so far had been fought.[2]

As the military fought a digital war on the battlefield, another, in embryo form, was taking place on the web.[3] Over this, a plethora of groups, organisations, governments, the military, NGOs (Non Government Organisations), old and new media and individuals from many nations released information, presented viewpoints and argued about the merits of the war. The web, with its global reach, its dynamic and interactive quality, and its openness to all, seemed to offer a new communication medium.[4] This was a medium that appeared to be truly democratic, allowing a voice to those often excluded from the mainstream.

In *Online Journalism*, Jim Hall suggests that the web offers a different paradigm for understanding the world around us, through its global feel, multimedia form, its provision of easy access to original sources, hyperlinks to provide context for stories, interactivity and the broader development of a discursive space. Hall notes:

> As the contenders [media organisations like MSNBC, CNN and BBC] battle it out they have produced news forms offering a depth that was largely absent in the traditional media. The capabilities of hypertext and multimedia forms, and the web's panoramic bandwidth, enable the coverage of stories in full context for the first time (books possibly excepted), with their histories, the social and technological forces that determine them and the economic trends and cultural tensions that drive them and emerge from them all represented.[5]

Using some of these categories above, plus a few more of my own, this essay will explore how the web provided a new more complex insight, perception and experience of the Iraqi war than that offered through the traditional media. Coming so soon after the war, this work should not be viewed as a sustained and in-depth piece of analysis. Instead, it is meant as a first reaction to the web coverage of the war; it is an attempt to mark out some of the issues and questions that will need to be researched further in future years.

Global feel

While the media has always been international in its reach, for example with news supplied by international news agencies or radio broadcasts across borders, the web allows a level and ease of communication across borders never seen before. If one is prepared to search for it, one can have access to information provided by a large range of different governments, national and international organisations, media bodies, corporate bodies and individuals from all nations. For example, throughout the war it was possible to visit a number of American media sites such as *CNN* (cnn.com), *Fox* (Fox.com), *The New York Times* (nytimes.com) and the *Washington Post* (washingtonpost.com) and to make comparisons between the coverage there and in the UK. Often the same story, written by the same journalist, would appear on sites on both sides of the Atlantic. On other occasions different concerns and areas of interest were evident. While *The Guardian,* for example, reported equally on what was happening with the American and British forces, the *New York Times* tended to focus much more on the US military. Also, from reading extensively stories on many British and American media sites, it could be suggested that the British press carried more critical stories, editorials and features than their American counterparts.

Anecdotally, it would seem that different views of the war were being provided; there is different copy for different societies. Thanks to the web, the ability to sample these sites, to drop in on other nation's media, is possible on a daily basis. No longer are you automatically confined by and to the national media, with its particular debates and viewpoints. While one can buy some foreign newspapers in Britain, and in this way sample news from around the world, it is much easier to access them through the web. From exploring and reading an array of international sources one can gain a much wider, and more complex, view of any conflict.[6]

In addition to these media sites there are other international resources that provide information and insight into how other cultures perceive and experience war. Thus, during the war, I logged onto the CIA site to find out background information about Iraq (http://www.cia.gov/cia/publications/factbook/), the Israel Ministry of Foreign Affairs (http://www.israel-mfa.gov.il/mfa/home.asp), the official Iranian government site (http://www.netiran.com/) and the UN's site (http://www.un.org/) to see what their positions were on the war; I also explored information offered about Iraq from an Arab perspective through the web site http://www.arab.net/iraq/. Indeed, as war loomed, many Americans, some 77 per cent of those with web access, used it to find out more about the Iraqi nation, society and its people from a variety of online sources.[7]

While governments and the military have historically tried to control the flow of information and communications between its citizens and others at times of war, they now find this increasingly hard. The web, with its ability to redirect information though multiple routes, is not the easiest media-communication form to control. Now the public can have access to the media and sources outside of their government's control, outside of their particular culture, even with the very country or countries with whom they are at war.

Horizontal communications

The web, with its ability to allow communications between one person and another, one to one, or between one person to many, has allowed the development of a form of communication not encouraged or usually allowed by the mass media. Rather than national journalists acting as mediators of what is happening in the world, one can communicate directly with other people about events occurring in their home towns and cities. The web allows a form of horizontal communication. One particularly interesting case of horizontal communication in the Iraqi war was that surrounding the Baghdad blogger – Salam Pax (www.dear_raed.blogspot.com). Pax, living in Baghdad, was able to provide an account of what it was like to witness and experience the war from the 'other' side, through his webblog, a form of personal diary. Of course it was hard, at first, to verify if this person did live in Baghdad, though many felt he was authentic.[8] By the week ending 23 March 2003, of the 316,000 people accessing Blogspot.com, some 86 per cent were visiting Salam Pax's site.[9] It might well be, as Erin Auerbach suggested before the outbreak of hostility, that, 'Web logs may be the CNN of the next war'.[10]

On the BBC's web site, like many other similar sites, the traditional media have tried to incorporate some form of this horizontal communications by including discussion areas where web users' comments are aired. These areas are often international in flavour as this extract taken from the BBC's website on 31 March 2003 illustrates:

> People in Britain have no idea what its (sic) like not to have simple freedom because it is not run under a medieval regime. You cannot have war without casualties, but is a small price to pay if it means restoring Iraq to the country it deserves to be and people can live with dignity and without fear.
>
> Vicky McLoughlin, England

> The US and UK have been shocked and awed. Never be arrogant and underestimate your enemy. Today Iraq is more united than before – a Stalingrad awaits the US and UK troops.
>
> Mehernosh, India

> I think it has. The main objective of this war is to keep Occidental public opinion quiet, which is working, and to bring civil disorder across the Middle East, which is on its way to working.
>
> Matthos, Rennes, France

> Initially I expected the defeat of the US (the UK would have dropped out by then) in six years. Now I am not even sure that the invaders will be able to sustain their losses in lives and credibility for six months. The idiocy of this war is mind boggling.
>
> Ronald Vopel, Belgium

Such a discussion illustrates how the web differs from traditional media. It allows a voice to people who often feel estranged by the media. It provides an international public space where debate can occur, almost instantaneously, with less selection and editing than usually happens with a paper's letter page. It facilitates a sharing of views from many different perspectives. Perhaps, 'the new electronic technologies are empowering citizens to participate in new democratic forums not only between government and the governed but also amongst citizens themselves'.[11]

Since the end of the war, announced, precipitately as it turned out, by President Bush on 1 May 2003, the dissatisfaction of many American soldiers has come to the public's notice. They are not happy to remain in Iraq being attacked and killed on an almost daily basis. This they have made known by emails sent back home to their families, some which have been posted, anonymously, on various sites, for example a web site run by David Hackworth, the youngest colonel to have served in the Vietnam war.[12] The usual attempt and capacity of the military to control communication from the front have now been eroded.[13] 'In a message posted on a website last week, one soldier was brutally frank. "Somewhere down the line, we became an occupation force in [Iraqi] eyes. We don't feel like heroes any more."'[14] The web has allowed an avenue of dissatisfaction not usually accessible until a long time after a conflict. Such feedback from the frontline has lead to intense pressure on politicians at home to 'bring the boys back'.

Interactivity

Whereas the mass media operates as a top down form of media, transmitting and distributing its output to a large number of people with little feedback possible, the web is a different creature. It is one that thrives on and invites interaction. Indeed, the traditional news companies, which had initially hoped to dominate the web by merely dumping their content on line, what Jim Hall calls 'Shovelware', fared badly and have had to think again.[15] While such content is useful and much sought after, the web requires it to be offered as part of a new form of interactive media. Web users expect to be offered hyperlinks to other sources and pages, whether on that site or not. They expect a mix of material on a site; often news pages will also have links to the weather and will include search facilities and TV and radio information. A new form of journalism is required, a form of 'People's Journalism',[16] which offers '[new] ways of exploiting the interactivity between reader, text and author'.[17] The user actively decides what they will look at, what route they will seek to explore the web. They expect to be able to express their views through polls and in discussion groups, to email journalists, indeed to affect the copy. Anamika Wani, section editor of *Online Journalism*, suggests that the traditional media should, in fact, use their websites in a different way to the physical copy; they could use it as a place for their more controversial images, a place where the reality of war is more truly shown.[18]

For example, if one looks at the CNN site for 3 April 2003, one finds the news coverage of the war presented in an interactive format. The CNN International page is dominated by a number of brief overviews of international stories about the war from around the world. Each one has a link to the full text. Alongside these, on the same page, is information about the financial markets, links to weather from around the world, access to a web search engine, a poll on whether world opinion would change if weapons of mass destruction were found, and the ability to email CNN. There is a sense, as one explores the site and, perhaps, as one explores links leading off site, that you are having a uniquely interactive experience. The user is able to forge their own path through the news, albeit within the bounds of the links provided. Of course the more adventurous you are as a user, the more unique your news experience. This is news in process. Likewise you do not just have to take in what is given to you, you can email back, vote or join in a discussion. Information directly given by you or collated from your use of the site will affect its design. You are interacting with this form of media, shaping and exploring your understanding of the Iraqi war.

Sources on the net

Journalists, in the past, have taken on the role of exploring many sources that were inaccessible for most of us. These they would summarise and critique for their audiences. What the web allows, however, has been a new means for web users, to visit many of the sources now found online. For example, in relation to the Iraqi war, one can visit the site, www.globalsecurity.org where, through the link 'Hot Sources', one can look at an array of briefing statements, transcripts of speeches and documents about the war. Using this you can move between newspaper reports, provided by journalists, and the original documents. You can compare and contrast the views and arguments being expressed with the document in question. One is empowered by the web. Suddenly, whole arrays of sources are at your fingertips whether they are official information from your government, from another government, from international organisations, protest sites or whatever. To borrow a comment made about the release of the Ken Starr report on the web, 'All the filters that are present in the world of journalism evaporated. Raw information was available in mainstream.'[19] It does not, however, mean that the journalist is no longer needed; they still have a role of sieving through all that is out there and analysing such material; but now we, the public, can, if we wish, look at the documents in their complete form. For example, at the time of writing, the Radio 4 *Today's* site allowed you to download the complete government's dossier of 24 Sept 2002 on *Iraq's Weapons of Mass Destruction*.[20]

Multimedia

While traditional newspapers and broadcast media offer certain combinations of media forms – text, speech or moving pictures – the web, at least in a limited form, offers all three in an interconnected interactive way. For example, the BBC's web site offered, at the time of the Iraqi war, not only text-based stories but also radio (aural) and television versions. The user can choose what to watch, listen to or read. While, because of technical limitations, the film pictures are grainy and not of broadcast quality, in time, as broadband is rolled out, such websites will offer a truly multimedia coverage of the war.

For example, on the CNN site, one could see how different media experiences of the war were presented. For 3 April 2003 (12:05 EST), the main lead story was

'Bush rallies Troops'. The user could, if they wished see more of this news story by selecting to view some of the videos on offer, 'Tanks on the Move' or 'Palace raid'. There were also links to maps and satellite photos of Iraqi, to a gallery of photos of the day and to CNN radio – though it must be noted that some of this access does require payment.

Hyperlinking/archiving

Traditional broadcast media are temporal. They are transmitted in a scheduled flow. One usually experiences them in an intended order, unless some form of recorder is used. Likewise newspapers, which are ephemeral, only offer access to recent stories. There is a temporal limitation to their coverage. Within both media forms references might be made to old stories; indeed, these older news stories might even be reprinted or retransmitted. The web, however, has not only a spatial bias, i.e. has global reach, it also has a temporal bias.[21] It is the perfect medium for accessing a huge range of contemporary and past stories. Newspapers, radio and TV broadcasters now archive their output, which, either free or through subscription, is mostly accessible to those with web access. Hyperlinks between stories allow a much more complex, less controlled picture of the war to appear. The user is able to follow different links, into the past or sideways, into other stories, media forms and other sites. The links might lead to audio or visual information, to chat sites or to non-news archives.

For example, the *Daily Telegraph's* site story, 'Missile "was not ours"' (filed on 4 April 2003) had a number of hyperlinks. They linked the story back to earlier coverage of when the missile hit on a Baghdad market place was first reported (filed on 29 March 2003).[22] The page also had an external link to the 10 Downing Street web site (http://www.number-10.gov.uk/output/Page1.asp), where the reader could learn how the British government was reacting to this event. While users' experiences of following stories have certain boundaries placed on them – the links provided are controlled and constrained by web designers – they can search further afield by using a search engine. For example, the Qatar based *Gulf Times* led on 29 March 2003 with the headline, 'Many die in market blast', presenting a more critical account of the explosion than the British press.[23]

The subversive

To end, I wish to suggest that the web can be a place of mischief, carnival, of fun and subversion. It is a place where official accounts, the accepted notions, can be turned on their head. For example, there are such sites as *The Onion* (www.theonion.com/predirect.html), 'America's finest news source', which adopts a satirical role, poking fun at journalistic practice, other news sources and the consensus. For example, they led on 26 March 2003 with a story entitled, 'Bush Bravely leads the 3rd infantry Division into battle'.[24] This plays with the current image of Bush and his gung-ho rhetoric and his past history of escaping the draft at the time of the Vietnam War.

Also, a spoof page appeared at about this time which is downloaded when searching, through Google, for 'weapons of mass destruction'. The page returned is similar to the one which appears when a sought after page cannot be found. The spoof page says things like, 'The weapons you are looking for are currently unavailable', where the page it mimics would say, 'The page you are looking for cannot be found'. It continues, 'The country might be experiencing technical difficulties, or you may need to adjust your weapons inspectors mandate.'[25] Between June and July the *Blueyonder* site, which hosted this page, gained, according to *Nielsen-Netrating*, a 1,240 per cent increase in viewing.[26]

As Baghdad fell, as Bush announced the end of the war, Saddam's minister of information, Mohamed Saeed al-Sharaf, was honoured with the setting up of a number of websites in homage to his work.[27] On these were quotations from his press briefings where, in rhetoric similar to Saddam Hussein, he would curse the infidels invading his country while ignoring the fact that Baghdad was being overrun. One infamous quotation read, 'There are no American [Pause for bomb explosion in background] infidels in Baghdad. NEVER!' As this was happening a coalition tank was clearly seen behind the information minister![28] Through the web he became an international star of the war, people read his quotes online and bought the tee shirts; a sign of fame if there was ever one. Following the appearance of these websites and the fan worship of Mohamed Saeed al-Sharaf, the world media took up the story.[29]

Conclusion: The digital future

The days when the military could control access to and information coming from the battlefront, when the news media would patriotically support the consensus, and when the public would mostly be behind the nation at a time of war, have now gone. The public are more critical, they want to know why their soldiers are going to die, why civilians will be killed and why destruction will take place. Certain sections of the public, even when the fighting had started in Iraq, continued to protest loudly about the war.[30] The demands for information, for news, the way the public come to understand war, the way they make sense of it, has changed hugely. No longer are they reliant on a compliant news media. Now they also have access to the web.

The military have started to respond to these developments. In the Iraqi war they increased their co-operation with reporters by offering lavish briefings at purpose-built media centres, and embedded some 700 journalists with frontline military units,[31] some of whom filed reports on the web. One could follow the daily experiences of the embedded BBC journalists through their personal 'weblogs', though they were called 'war diaries' on the BBC's website. Alongside such increased 'co-operation' with the press, the military have also started to run their own web sites.[32] Web users no longer need depend on the media to report on the military briefings for up-to-date information; they can, if they so wish, go to the military sites to find out what is happening.

The military are developing their digital capabilities both on the battlefield and on the information front. Increasingly, the military are orientating themselves to providing more information to web users – individuals or journalists. As the web becomes more important, as it offers more potential, the military will take this into account as they design their media strategies for the coming wars.

Indeed, if one wants to speculate further, it might seem as if there is a point at which the military digital command system, which collects and collates information about what is happening on the battlefield, might come to overlap with the web, the civilian digital network. As the military become tied to the demands of the public, as they seek to win an almost continual plebiscite, the web offers them a direct communication line with their citizens. Rather than relying on the media to question the truth of events on the frontline, the military can, within certain limits, allow citizens to tap into the military's real time intelligence flows. Why can't the citizens who send the military to war watch what they are doing in their name? Why can't the public see, within reason, what the generals are watching? Why can't we experience the virtual simulation of the war, like our commanders? Why can't we all be our own generals, receiving the same input, and then deciding, by some electronic vote, if we want our armies to continue in the field? This might be far fetched, but, a few years ago, so too would be the idea that you could watch, live, your missiles landing upon the enemy. While the technologies of war have changed, so has the importance and role of the public. The culture of militarism, where the military gained automatic support from the nation's public, has been challenged by the huge protests that happened before and during the Iraqi war. Increasingly, the public feel they really do have a right and duty to keep a check on what the military do in their name. The web offers the means of doing this.

Notes

1. To avoid confusion the earlier war of 1991 will be referred to as the Gulf war and that of 2003 as the Iraqi war. It should be noted that for some commentators, it might be disputable whether this conflict, like the Gulf war, could be called a war; perhaps it is more of a massacre between two unequal factions). Of course, some, Jim Hall for example, argue that Kosovo was the first web war. We wait to find out what the historical records of these two wars will say of the importance of the web (Jim Hall, *Online Journalism: A Critical Primer*, Pluto Press, London 2001, pp94-127).

2. Randeep Ramesh (Ed.), *The War We Could Not Stop: The real story of the battle for Iraq*, Faber and Faber, London 2003, pp240-46. Though it should be noted that the most advanced digital soldiers, those of the 4th Infantry (the digital brigade), spent most of the war unsuccessfully trying to enter Iraq.

3. According to nua surveys (www.nua.com), there are currently some 605.60m with access world wide to the web. Of these, 6.31m are in Africa, 187.24m in Asia/pacific rim, 190.91m in Europe, 5.12m in the Middle East, 182.67m in Canada/ USA and 33.35m in Latin America.

4. Sean Dodson, 'Brutal reality hits home', *Guardian*, 21 August 2003.

5. Jim Hall, *Online Journalism: A Critical Primer*, Pluto Press, London 2001, p227.

6. A good site for finding newspapers from around the world is www.newsdirectory.com.

7. Lee Rainie et al, *The Internet and the Iraqi war: How online America have used the internet to learn war news, understand events and promote their news*, Pew Internet and American Life Project, Washington 2003.

8. Randeep Ramesh (Ed.), op cit, p264-5.

9. www.Nielsen-netrating.com.

10. Erin Auerbach, 'Web logs may be the CNN of the next war', OnlineJournalism.com, 8 December 2002.

11. Howard Tumber, 'Democracy in the information age: The role of the fourth estate in Cyberspace', in *Information, Communication and Society*, 4:1 2001, pp95-112.

12. www.hackworth.com.

13. There was some attempt at limiting soldiers' access to email and monitoring their emails: Erin Auerbach, 'Soldiers' emails from the Gulf may be monitored', Onlinejournalism.com, 12 March 2003.

14. P. Harris and J. Franklin, ' "Bring us home": GIs flood US with war-weary emails', *The Observer*, 10 August 2003.

15. Jim Hall, op cit, pp28-32.

16. S. Yelvington quoted in Howard Tumber, op cit, pp95-112.

17. Jim Hall, op cit, p29.

18. Anamika Wani, 'Show the reality of war online, differentiate from print', OnlineJournalism.com, 18 April 2003.

19. Michael McCurry, 'The President's Scorpions', *Correspondent*, BBC2 31 October 1998, quoted in Howard Tumber, op cit, p104.

20. http://www.bbc.co.uk/radio4/today/reports/archive/international/iraqdossier.pdf .

21. Harold Innis, *Empire and Communications*, University of Toronto Press, Toronto 1950.

22. Michael Smith and Neil Tweedie, 'Baghdad market bomb kills 55', *Telegraph*, 29 March 2003.

23. http://www.newsdirectory.com/go/?f=andr=asandu=www.gulf-times.com.

24. http://www.theonion.com/onion3911/bush_bravely_leads.html.

25. http://www.coxar.pwp.blueyonder.co.uk.

26. As reported in City Diary in the *Guardian*, 21 August 2003.

27. http://www.freecrap.co.uk/iraqi/whereishe.html.

28. http://www.freecrap.co.uk/iraqi/quotes.html.

29. Larry Elliott (2003) 'Sceptics start sniping al-Gordon', in *The Guardian*, 28 April 2003 .

30. Randeep Ramesh (Ed.), op cit, pp71-79.

31. http://www.defenselink.mil/news/Jan2003/t01152003_t0114bc.html.

32. For example, the MOD has www.mod.uk, the royal navy, www.royal-navy.mod.uk, army, www.army-mod.uk and the Royal Airforce, www.raf.mod.uk .

The *Daily Mirror* and the war on Iraq

Des Freedman

This article examines the remarkable coverage of the Iraq war by the Daily Mirror, *which acted as a focal point of anti-war sentiment in Britain. Its controversial attitude was part of its efforts to rebrand itself as a serious yet popular read. The* Mirror's *motivations reflected a desire both to connect with the millions who were against the war and to carve out a distinct identity for itself in order to better compete with its main tabloid rival, the* Sun. *Its coverage demonstrates that radical and accessible journalism is possible during periods of social crisis but that commercial newspapers are highly unstable vehicles for such a project.*

Introduction

'You are NOT powerless, You DO have a voice' argued the British tabloid newspaper the *Daily Mirror* (*DM*) on its front page, just above the headline of NO WAR. On that day, 21 January 2003, the newspaper launched its petition to Prime Minister Tony Blair opposing the proposed war on Iraq, a petition that was eventually signed by over 220,000 people. The *Mirror* campaigned tirelessly to rebut the arguments of the British and US administrations that sought to justify a war, and employed the talents of leading political journalists like John Pilger and Jonathan Freedland to make the anti-war case. Celebrity gossip and scandal, once the staple of the *Mirror's* news agenda, were kicked off the front page to be replaced by hard-hitting critiques of the pro-war lobby. Having backed the Stop the War Coalition's two million-strong demonstration in London on 15 February 2003, the newspaper provided for its readers on the following Monday 'a historic 12-page picture souvenir of our greatest-ever protest march'. Memories of Royal Jubilees, Cup Finals and *Big Brother* seemed a long way off.

Once the war started, the *Mirror* adopted a more cautious political position. It maintained opposition to the war itself but focused more on celebrating the courage and dedication of British soldiers. As the conflict continued, its coverage and editorial position became less distinctive, reducing its identification with the anti-war movement, curtailing its criticism of Tony Blair and returning gossip and showbiz news to more prominent positions in the paper. On 11 April, it was revealed that the *Mirror's* circulation had dropped below the key psychological barrier of two million copies a day, while its main rival, the pro-war *Sun*, had actually added readers during the war. The following morning saw the paper's first non-war related front page since the beginning of March and the emergence of a more 'balanced' news agenda, juggling celebrity stories, domestic news and the aftermath of the Iraq war.

This chapter examines the *Mirror's* behaviour in the build-up to and in the course of the war on Iraq. By adopting a highly politicised anti-government stance and by encouraging its readers to be active opponents of the war, the *Mirror* confounded the typical model of the tabloid newspaper as a repository of gossip, and the tabloid reader as a depoliticised, conservative, passive figure. The chapter highlights the constraints facing such a project in the light of the paper's ultimate ambition to make profits for its corporate owners at Trinity Mirror plc and, finally, reflects on the possibilities for and limitations of oppositional media practices in the context of a competitive 'free press' system.

Rebranding the Mirror

The *Mirror's* public and very determined opposition to the war was unprecedented. While the paper supported British involvement in two of the most recent conflicts, the 1991 Gulf War and the 1999 campaign in Kosovo, it also has a long-established anti-war tradition, having opposed both the Suez invasion in 1956 and the Falklands War in 1982. But in opposing the war in Iraq, the *Mirror* was confronting the military plans of a *Labour* government for the first time and was in danger of alienating the Labour supporters who formed the core of its readership. According to David Seymour, the Mirror Group's political editor and leader writer, 'you have to remember who *Mirror* readers are. The *Mirror* was traditionally ▶ right-wing Labour because the readers were right-wing Labour and it walked a fine line in all of that.' Some of the paper's coverage of Iraq was, according to Seymour, 'in hindsight, very close to the line, if not over it'.[1]

At another level, the *Mirror's* anti-war stance could be seen as the logical conclusion of a rebranding exercise that had started following the events of 9/11 and the perceived desire amongst the reading public for a more analytical approach to news in order to understand both the roots and dangers of terrorism. Piers Morgan, the *Mirror's* editor, shifted the paper away from an unremitting emphasis on celebrity scandal and human interest stories towards a focus on international coverage that included a particularly critical stance towards the US and UK bombing of Afghanistan in late 2001. This approach was consolidated with the £19.5 million formal relaunch of the *Mirror* in April 2002 when the paper's traditional 'red top' masthead was exchanged for a more

sombre black one and 'heavyweight' journalists like John Pilger (the leading
investigative reporter and long-time *Mirror* writer), *Vanity Fair's* Christopher
Hitchens and the *Guardian's* Jonathan Freedland were all given regular
columns. According to Morgan, the changes were all about the *Mirror*
becoming a 'serious paper with serious news, serious sport, serious gossip and
serious entertainment' (*DM*, 16 April 2002). While sport, gossip and
entertainment were common features of all tabloid papers, Morgan gambled
that one way to distinguish the *Mirror* from its rivals would be to adopt a
broadly left-wing, 'Old Labour' position that challenged both the domestic and
international perspectives of the New Labour government. This was an unusual
form of 'product differentiation' – a phenomenon more often consisting of
'scoops', competitions and giveaways – but not an entirely unreasonable one
given signs of growing resistance to the Blair government. David Seymour
argues that the move 'upmarket' was certainly in response to 9/11 but also
reflected a more general critical engagement with the Blair government, as 'the
Mirror is more radical now than it's ever been'.[2]

The relaunch and new radical tone was not just in response to a changed
political climate but also was a much-needed measure to address the long-term
circulation decline of the *Mirror* and to close the gap with its principal
competitor, the *Sun*.[3] In May 2002, the *Mirror* (averaging around 2.1 million
copies a day) cut its price from thirty-two to twenty pence a day in order to steal
readers from the *Sun* (average circulation around 3.5 million copies a day). The
latter's response was swift and vicious: an even more substantial price cut that
neutralised the *Mirror's* move and cost both titles an enormous amount of money,
a situation that the *Sun* was more able to bear given the deep pockets of its owner,
Rupert Murdoch's News International. By the end of 2002, neither the price-cuts
nor the more radical news agenda had stopped the decline in sales, which were
hovering just above the two million mark.

The relaunch of 2001/2 was the latest in a long line of *Mirror* 'rebranding'
exercises. The newspaper was founded in 1903 as a 'boudoir paper for – and
produced by – women',[4] but when that format proved to be unsuccessful, it rapidly
turned into a Liberal-supporting 'picture paper'. In the 1930s, the *Mirror* was
further transformed into a socially aware, mass-circulation tabloid specifically
aimed at workers. The decision to throw its weight behind Labour in the following
decade was, according to one historian, taken as 'little more than a marketing
calculation that its appeal to a working-class audience meant that [in the words of
Mirror chairman Cecil King] "the politics had to be made to match".'[5]

When the Conservatives won three successive elections in the 1950s, the
Mirror was once again forced to adapt to new circumstances. James Curran
argues that the paper watered down the class rhetoric of the 1940s and took on
a more middle-of-the-road political stance in order to attract the 'young and

upwardly mobile readers' sought by advertisers.[6] Finally, the recently-appointed editor Piers Morgan oversaw a £16 million relaunch in 1997 which sought to modernise the *Mirror*, adding colour, celebrity features and 'racy' front pages that would position it as the 'paper for the new millennium'. This attempt to invigorate and renew the paper's readership was most graphically illustrated by the controversy surrounding Morgan's choice of ACHTUNG! SURRENDER! as the cover story on the day of a football match between England and Germany in the 1996 European Championship. According to Morgan, 'the Achtung thing was as joke that people didn't get, that's all. We did it to get the youth on side. We've got droves of readers over sixty-five. We've gotta get the youth.'[7]

These continuous rebranding exercises demonstrate the uncertainties of the political and economic environment in which the *Mirror* finds itself. It has long held progressive views that threaten to alienate advertisers; it has based itself on an identification with a single political party whose own fortunes have fluctuated and whose supporters have aged thus making them less attractive to advertisers. At a time when party political affiliations are declining, the *Mirror* is still the paper with, by far, the most loyal political base – 71 per cent of *Mirror* readers voted Labour in the 2001 general election, six per cent more than the number of *Telegraph* readers who voted Conservative.[8] In an increasingly competitive market, therefore, the politics of a particular newspaper title are bound to be more tactical than ever, determined partly by editorial tradition, proprietorial intervention and marketing assumptions concerning how to connect with the opinions and interests of the target audience.

The Mirror and the build–up to war

The *Mirror* followed up its hostility towards the British and American bombing of Afghanistan in 2001 with a series of articles that warned against going to war with Iraq as a distraction from the real fight against international terrorism. The problems involved in challenging George Bush and Tony Blair's war plans soon became clear. The *Mirror* celebrated American Independence Day with the headline MOURN ON THE FOURTH OF JULY (*DM*, 4 July 2002, figure one) and a two-page article by John Pilger that described the US as 'the world's leading rogue state ... out to control the world'. In response, the fund manager of one of Trinity Mirror's large American investors, Tweedy Browne, phoned up the *Mirror's* chief executive to complain about the article. According to Roy Greenslade in the *Guardian*, the fund manager

> told me he had simply wanted to register his disappointment about the *Daily Mirror's* coverage to its owners. He stressed that he had opened his remarks by saying he was

strongly committed to the freedom of the press but that the 'right' to that freedom required that it be used responsibly and fairly. 'The *Mirror* wasn't fair and wasn't accurate,' he said.

(*Guardian*, 15 July 2002).

Morgan defended Pilger and emphasised his popularity with *Mirror* readers (if not American investors) but the episode showed that an anti-Bush, let alone an anti-imperialist, position would generate real flak.

Through the rest of the year, the paper developed its argument that an attack on Iraq would be counter-productive and would 'make us less secure, not more' (*DM*, 1 January 2003). Responding to opinion polls showing a lack of popular support for an invasion of Iraq, the *Mirror* attempted to articulate this anti-war sentiment in bold and imaginative ways. On 6 January, the paper adapted a cartoon by US labour cartoonist Gary Huck, that suggested that Bush's motive for attacking Iraq lay with his desire to control oil resources in the region, and ran it on the front page (see figure two). As preparations for war intensified, the *Mirror* escalated its own anti-war profile by launching its 'No War' petition – that allowed it to feature pictures of celebrities signing the petition every day – and distributing a free 'No War' poster. The first six or so pages of the paper each morning became devoted to the subject of the impending war and how to resist it. Morgan sanctioned further polemical, campaigning and highly controversial

Figure 1

Figure 2

front pages, including one featuring Blair with BLOOD ON HIS HANDS (*DM*, 29 January 2003, figure three) that David Seymour remembers as being particularly 'close to the line'.

Figure 3

The *Mirror* did not simply challenge the arguments for going to war but helped to mobilise opposition to the US and UK governments. It reported on the global anti-war protests in January and firmly identified itself with the national demonstration due to take place in London on 15 February. Two days before, it published a four-page guide to the march that included a map of the route and contact details of local transport to get to London. The *Mirror* paid for the video screen in Hyde Park at the end of the march and printed thousands of 'No War' placards with the paper's logo at the top. Such was the enthusiasm for the protest amongst ordinary *Mirror* staff, according to David Seymour, that many turned up to distribute the placards and to participate in the march. 'There was a strong feeling that we were on the side of right and standing up against not just the government, particularly the Bush government, and against the might of the rest of the press.'[9] The following Monday, the paper featured ten pages on preparations for war as well as a twelve-page commemorative report on the protest march. By the time the war started, the *Mirror* was devoting up to fifteen pages a day in a popular tabloid condemning the arguments of the US and UK administrations and urging the public to raise its voice against a war.

The *Mirror's* coverage in the early part of 2003 failed to stem the decline in circulation but did, at least, win it critical acclaim and much-needed publicity.[10] Seymour recalls that the anti-war position was 'overwhelmingly supported by the readers' and that editorial staff were encouraged by opinion polls showing an anti-war majority in the UK.

> I was at a conference with the political editor of the *Sun* in the run-up to war and he said to me 'how many readers have you lost because of your stance on Iraq?' I said 'why should we lose readers when what we're saying is what the British public is saying?' It was the *Sun* that was flying in the face of British public opinion.[11]

This confidence encouraged the *Mirror* to venture into other controversial areas, most notably over the issue of asylum seekers and refugees. On 20 January, the paper ran a full-page feature on 'Why immigration is good for Britain' and followed this up in early March with a three-page special exposing the myths and reality about asylum seekers and pointing out Britain's poor record of accepting refugees despite the contribution they make to the country (*DM*, 3 March 2003). The *Mirror* was, for a time, the model of an accessible, popular, campaigning and challenging daily newspaper.

There were some ambiguities in the *Mirror's* anti-war position, particularly in its attitude towards Tony Blair. One day it would accuse Blair of 'breathtaking arrogance' for ignoring a potential United Nations veto (*DM*, 7 March 2003) while the next it would admire Blair's resilience. 'Tony Blair has been the strongest and most powerful prime minister of modern times ... He started down this road [of war] with the best intentions. But he has found himself in a dead end' (*DM*, 12 March 2003). The conclusion was that Blair was an admirable and determined leader who was making a tactical mistake in allying himself with the real cowboy, George Bush. Furthermore, the *Mirror's* opposition to a war did not include the withdrawal of support for British troops should they be involved. Two days before the war started, Seymour wrote a two-page leader in which he attacked the idea of war without international backing but added that our troops 'need to understand very clearly that once the fighting begins, the Daily Mirror unequivocally supports them' (*DM*, 18 March 2003).

This contradiction – of supporting the army but opposing the war – echoed a deeper political ambiguity about how best to secure British interests. Seymour argues that 'had the circumstances and timing been different, we would have supported military action to remove Saddam'. The problem was this was a US-led initiative led by 'warmongers' who wanted to seek revenge for 9/11. 'We just couldn't see what the advantages of going in like that in the way they did go in. Had there been a grand alliance of nations as there had been after 9/11, I think it would have been difficult for us to completely oppose it.'[12] In the run-up to the war, the isolation of the British and US administrations, together with public backing for the anti-war position, was enough to convince Piers Morgan and David Seymour that opposition was justified and that pursuing an anti-war position was in the *Mirror's* interest. To what extent would this last once the war had started?

The Mirror during the war

The *Mirror* continued to provide a voice for the anti-war movement even when British and American troops launched their invasion of Iraq on 20 March. Despite, or perhaps because of, the jingoistic coverage of its main competitors, the paper refused to change its opinion that the war was illegal and unjustified. Faced with accusations that to be against the war was unpatriotic, the *Mirror* filled its front page on 24 March with pictures of innocent civilian casualties and the headline STILL ANTI-WAR? YES, BLOODY RIGHT WE ARE! Along with a minority of other papers like the *Guardian* and *Independent*, the *Mirror* carried regular reports that condemned US and UK propaganda, the bombing of civilians, the appalling conditions in Baghdad and the instances of 'friendly fire'. It hired the veteran war reporter Peter Arnett, who had been sacked from MSNBC for speaking to state-run Iraqi TV, and turned this into a front page: 'Fired by America for telling the truth … Hired by the Mirror to carry on telling it' (*DM*, 1 April 2003). Between fifteen and twenty pages of an eighty-page tabloid newspaper were devoted to covering the war from a perspective that was generally critical of Blair and Bush's motivations.

Yet there were many areas in which the *Mirror's* coverage dovetailed with that of the rest of the press, particularly in focusing on the details of war. The paper ran a daily 'BATTLE TIMETABLE' filled with *Boy's Own* graphics, and aired the military analysis of former SAS soldier and thriller writer Andy McNab. The *Mirror* also went along with the highly problematic system of 'embedding' journalists inside military units. Tom Newton Dunn, embedded with forty Commando, provided regular reports of the bravery and benevolence of British troops as they 'pacified' southern Iraq. In a fairly typical report, Dunn describes a conversation during the 'liberation' of a small town called Abu Al Khasib as follows:

> 'What's your name?' asks one teenage boy wearing a tatty Inter Milan football shirt. 'You should be wearing a Manchester United shirt,' says Sgt Gary Evans, 31, from Chester, pulling out a packet of energy-packed sweets. 'Here you go son, have one of these. We've come to be your friends.' The locals speak only the odd word or phrase of English but the boy didn't need to understand, he just smiled.

This valorisation of British troops was the most visible evidence of a change of emphasis for the *Mirror*. Once the war had started, it was no longer seen as appropriate to undermine British military objectives and risk sapping troop morale. Readers' letters opposing the war were replaced by messages to the troops from family members and an increasing number of stories reporting on the success of the military campaign or praising the initiative of British soldiers. David Seymour argues that the *Mirror* was simply reflecting a shift in public attitudes. 'Since Suez, the accepted wisdom is that however much you campaign against military action, once it's started you have to fall in line behind your troops.'[13] Piers Morgan goes further, claiming that the *Mirror's* coverage *had* to change.

I personally slightly misjudged the way that you could be attitudinal on the front page in the way that we were, once the war actually started … I have never seen such a switch in public opinion … It's entirely down to the natural sense in this country – particularly among the tabloid readership – that once a war starts, if we're involved, we must unequivocally support our boys and girls.[14]

This was not the reaction of the hundreds of thousands of people who took direct action and marched demanding an immediate end to the war. The *Mirror*, at least initially, reflected *both* responses. On the day bombing started, Seymour's leader spoke of a 'horrible sense of helplessness for everyone back home here in Britain. All we can do is watch the television news and entrust our military leaders to do their job efficiently, speedily.' Yet over the page, John Pilger reported on the resistance to war, giving full details of protest groups and activities, under the headline of 'So what can YOU do? The polite term is civil disobedience … and the street term is rebellion' (*DM*, 20 March 2003). Yet when half a million people protested in London later that week – the biggest ever demonstration in Britain during wartime – there was no twelve-page supplement welcoming it but an attack from the *Mirror's* regular Monday columnist Tony Parsons: 'Being against this war when British soldiers are fighting and dying seems cheap, grubby and inappropriate' (*DM*, 24 March 2003).

Another area in which the ambiguities of the *Mirror's* political position were intensified by the outbreak of war concerned its attitude to Blair. Having previously accused Blair of having 'blood on his hands' and of being a 'PRIME MONSTER' (*DM*, 14 March 2003), the paper praised the 'passion and conviction' with which Blair addressed the nation and 'justified sending thousands of British troops into war' (*DM*, 21 March 2003). After a month of war, the paper was even more effusive. 'The past few months have seen Tony Blair unshakeably hold to the courage of his convictions … he has shown remarkable courage and leadership … he is entitled to receive recognition of his single-minded determination and relentless pursuit of his convictions' (*DM*, 17 April 2003). According to leader writer David Seymour:

My feeling, which Piers [Morgan] supported, was that even if we thought that Blair was wrong, it would be wrong for us to deliberately accuse him of lying. We never accused him of lying over weapons of mass destruction since the story broke. We've always been at pains to make the separation between misleading and downright lying. But I also thought that just as you need to support your troops in time of war, I think there would have been a real problem – particularly for the *Mirror* with the most Labour-supporting readers – to have attacked Blair, a Labour prime minister in the middle of the war.[15]

The *Mirror's* solution to the dilemma of how to connect to anti-war sentiment without alienating British troops (and readers) was to distinguish between what it saw as the honourable (if misguided) objectives of Tony Blair and the dishonourable, imperial ambitions of President Bush. The paper's front page on March 27 addressed Bush's love of war in no uncertain terms. 'Dead British troops paraded on Iraqi TV, 14 civilians killed in Baghdad market and Bush whoops it up. War? HE LOVES IT' (see figure four). A *Mirror* editorial followed this up by arguing that 'Blair's stand will help win the peace' and praised Blair for standing up to

Figure 4

Bush by insisting on a United Nations presence in Iraq and arguing against military action in Syria and Iran. The 'poodle' has turned into a 'terrier' (*DM*, 3 April 2003). The continuing agreement between George Bush and Tony Blair over weapons of mass destruction and the rationale for war in Iraq suggests that no such canine transformation ever took place.

These changes in the *Mirror's* coverage were stimulated not so much by a perception of a general shift in public opinion as by evidence that the paper's circulation was still declining. 'Do I think our anti-war line is to blame for any of the drop?' asked Morgan. 'Possibly a bit among our older readers who think it's unpatriotic to continue criticising the war now it's started. But the overwhelming reaction to our coverage from our readers has been totally supportive.'[16] However, a poll published in the *Guardian* on 31 March showed that while 38 per cent of *Mirror* readers disapproved of the military attack, 49 per cent approved of it.[17] Worse news was to follow. On 11 April it was revealed that the *Mirror's* circulation had fallen below the two million mark and that its anti-war stance had contributed to this decline. Morgan was clearly under great pressure to 'ameliorate'[18] the coverage, to lessen the paper's critical attitude to the war and to shift the war off the front pages and restore a more traditional tabloid balance of hard news and celebrity stories. Commercial considerations dominated over political principles.

Seymour claims that it was not the anti-war position but simply wall-to-wall coverage of the war itself that was the problem for the *Mirror*. He argues that the change wasn't about politics. We're in the business – amongst other things – of wanting people to read our newspaper. And a newspaper which is so unremittingly negative or grey is not going to do the job we want it to and it's not just selling copies, it's also getting a message over … The *Mirror* is a mass market product which is read by five million people every day and you have to be very very careful not to offend or turn off too many people.[19]

Hard-hitting anti-war covers were therefore replaced with ones attacking Saddam Hussein (SADDAM CHEEK, April 5), marking the courage of British soldiers (BORN TO SERVE, April 8) or celebrating military success (STATUE OF LIBERTY on the fall of Baghdad, April 10). Five front pages inside two weeks were devoted to the *Mirror's* campaign to help twelve-year-old Ali Abbas, who lost his family and both arms in an American bombing raid on Baghdad, to seek medical attention in the UK. 'What the Ali story did', according to Seymour, 'was it humanised the conflict.' Ali was one way of covering the war but in such a way as 'not to make it appear so negative'.[20] The Ali appeal was certainly well intentioned but it signalled an approach to the war with which Tony Blair and the rest of the British press could scarcely have disagreed. By 12 April, two days after the collapse of the Iraqi regime, the war had disappeared off the front page entirely to be replaced by a photograph of television personality Ulrika Johnsson and a story about the Prime Minister appearing on an edition of *The Simpsons*.

In the months following the war, the *Mirror* has returned to a more familiar look where celebrity surveillance shares the limelight with the aftermath of the invasion and other (mostly domestic) news stories. The coverage of Iraq continues to be more critical and thoughtful than most of the rest of the British press but the project to make the *Mirror* into a distinctive and socially aware popular tabloid appears to be somewhat half-hearted and fragile. *Mirror* readers are now more likely to be addressed in terms of their leisure interests than their political aspirations, while the imaginative features on asylum seekers have been replaced by a more traditional tabloid interest in crime (see figure five for a cover that combines celebrity, crime, fashion and

Figure 5

royalty). The well-established tabloid balance between 'soft' and 'hard' news has been resuscitated, the radical rhetoric tamed and corporate nerves soothed by a small increase in circulation.

Conclusions

There are some key lessons about the role of the press to be learned from the *Mirror's* performance during the Iraq war. The first is that at a time of profound social crisis when elites are divided amongst themselves and the public is willing to challenge and mobilise against these elites, a space can open up in which radical ideas start to circulate. In the context of a mass movement against Tony Blair's attempt to involve Britain in a US-led invasion of Iraq and serious international disagreement about the legitimacy of such military action, the *Mirror* was able to articulate and reinforce the views of this movement and to air opinions that would otherwise have been marginalised in the mainstream media. When the movement was on the up in the months preceding an invasion, the *Mirror* was happy to draw on a wide range of anti-war voices and to organise opposition to an invasion. It shifted from a newspaper that addressed its readers in fairly passive and restricted terms to one in which readers were conceptualised as active, thoughtful and capable of making an informed contribution to both the paper and the wider world. The significance of a mass-circulation tabloid newspaper taking on such a perspective should not be underestimated.

Although the *Mirror's* circulation continued to decline during the war (which still involved some two million people choosing to buy a radical, anti-war paper every day), there is little evidence that its position on the war was the main contributor. David Seymour argues that, while some people did stop buying the paper because of the anti-war stance, others started taking it precisely *because* of its views. 'I got quite a lot e-mail from people who said "I used to be a *Sun* reader but I switched to the *Mirror* because you've got a good attitude to the war"'.[21] For Seymour and other media commentators, the precise political inflection of a tabloid paper is less of a factor in sales than its price. For the whole period leading up to and during the war, the *Sun* was able to maintain a price differential and therefore buy its way into a widening sales gap between the two papers. In any case, according to former *Guardian* editor Peter Preston, Trinity Mirror should have expected a decline in sales as one of the consequences of trying to push the *Mirror* upmarket. Rebranding, or as Preston calls it 'resurrection by differentiation', takes time, especially when it involves a serious attempt to win new and different readers. 'This is real long haul territory, with a smaller but better-resourced readership for advertisers at the end of journey. It needs resources, dedication, heavy marketing – and the management will to change the *Mirror's* core identity over a decade.'[22] In the end, the *Mirror's* anti-war position proved to be a convenient scapegoat for critics (inside and outside Trinity Mirror) who were demanding editorial changes, even though more money was lost in the fruitless price-cutting exercise with the *Sun*[23] than in the small decline in sales over the period of the war.

When 'differentiation' takes a highly political form that has already antagonised investors, shareholders and government itself, it becomes clear that a newspaper whose ultimate responsibility is to make a profit is not a reliable ally for a radical anti-war movement. Although the *Mirror* was initially keen to express the overwhelming anti-war sentiment in the UK, when military action started and opinion polls revealed a more ambivalent attitude towards the war amongst both its own readers and the general public, the *Mirror* was less willing to be identified with what it saw as minority views. Constrained by a 'responsibility' towards the bottom line, the paper was unable to maintain a consistent opposition towards the war and was forced to 'ameliorate' its coverage. Such is the logic of the newspaper business. Moments of social crisis can open up spaces for innovative and radical coverage but they sit uneasily with the market disciplines of a 'free press' that privilege, above all, profitability and competitiveness.

Notes

1. David Seymour, interview with the author, 14 July 2003.
2. Ibid.
3. The *Mirror's* circulation peaked at over five million in the mid-1960s but declined following the relaunch by Rupert Murdoch of the *Sun*.
4. Colin Seymour Ure, 'Northcliffe's Legacy', in Peter Catterall, Colin Seymour-Ure and Anthony Smith (Eds), *Northcliffe's Legacy: Aspects of the British Popular Press, 1896-1996*, Macmillan, London 2000, p10.
5. James Thomas, 'The "Max Factor" – a Mirror Image? Robert Maxwell and the *Daily Mirror* tradition', in ibid, p214.
6. James Curran and Jean Seaton, *Power Without Responsibility*, Routledge, London 1991, p111. Curiously this 'deradicalisation' is the precise opposite of the most recent example of the *Mirror's* rebranding where 'radical politics' was seen to be a central plank of the strategy of product differentiation.
7. John Pilger, *Hidden Agendas*, Vintage, London 1998, p438.
8. MORI poll, 'How Britain Voted in 2001', 20 July 2001, available at www.mori.com/polls/2001/elections.html.
9. Seymour, op cit. Despite huge popular opposition to a war, the bulk of the British daily press supported the proposed attack. It was predictable that the News International and Hollinger titles would line up behind a war given the ideological preferences of their proprietors (Rupert Murdoch and Conrad Black respectively), but the decision of the more liberal-minded *Observer* to support Tony Blair was more surprising – possibly stemming from a desire not to lose circulation as it had when the paper opposed the British occupation of Suez in 1956.
10. The *Guardian* (17 February 2003) reported that the *Mirror* gained £100,000 worth of free publicity with its sponsorship of the 15 February demonstration. 'Thousands of marchers carried Daily Mirror "No War" posters on Saturday, resulting in a double whammy of brand promotion among the 1 million-strong crowd and in news coverage on TV and press.'

11. Seymour, op cit.
12. Ibid.
13. Ibid.
14. Quoted in Ian Burrell, 'Morgan's dilemma', *Belfast Telegraph*, April 2003, available at http://www.belfasttelegraph.co.uk/iraqcrisis/uknews124.jsp.
15. Seymour, op cit.
16. Owen Gibson, 'Mirror readers turn off war stance', *The Guardian*, 3 April 2003.
17. Poll results are at www.IMAGE.Guardian.co.uk/sysfiles/politics/documents/2003/03/25/03251CM.pdf.
18. Seymour, op cit.
19. Ibid.
20. Ibid.
21. Ibid.
22. Peter Preston, 'Bore-bore not war-war is turn-off', The *Guardian*, 3 April 2003.
23. Price-cutting cost Trinity Mirror £23.5 million in 2002 alone (Trinity Mirror plc, *Annual Report and Accounts 2002*, p13).

Reporting Iraq – what went right? what went wrong?

Jake Lynch

This article is based on the transcript of a discussion held among senior London-based journalists organised by Reporting the World, the journalism think-tank, on 15 July 2003.

Introduction

The case for invading Iraq remained a matter of public concern in the aggressor countries – the US, UK, Spain and Australia – to an extent unmatched before, during or, particularly, after any other war in recent times.

Echoing this was an audible level of disquiet among journalists. Many who had reported from Iraq, or spent the period leading up to and spanning the war in charge of papers or newsdesks, joined in a discussion about the coverage – both in print and in person – which, again, was unprecedented in both scope and tone.

One gathering of editors and senior correspondents convened in London under the auspices of the *Media Guardian*. Then Michael Wolff, media critic of *New York Magazine*, chaired a similar meeting in New York. In a report of proceedings, he observed how recriminations over the conduct and coverage of the war were now feeding off each other:

> Clearly, the war will be more of a story. It gets bigger every day. Not least of all because the media is now having to rewrite itself. The questions we failed to ask, the stories we declined to pursue, have surely helped to get us into the present mess.

Reporting the world

In London, on 15 July 2003, probably the most senior of these gatherings took place under the banner of Reporting the World (RtW), in conjunction with the security think-tanks, Saferworld, BASIC (British-American Security Information Council) and ISIS (International Security Information Service).

Conceived as a series of discussions, publications and a website (www.reportingtheworld.org) mainly for UK journalists, on the ethics of covering conflicts, the *Observer* newspaper described Reporting the World as 'the nearest thing we have to a journalism think-tank'.

On this occasion, the discussion, chaired by Annabel McGoldrick, was titled *Reporting Iraq – what went right? What went wrong?* Participants included the Editor of the *Guardian*; Heads of News from both the BBC and CNN International; Foreign Editors of the *Times* and *Guardian*, Group Political Editor of the *Mirror* and several distinguished correspondents who followed events either in Baghdad or in embedded positions with forward units.

What follows is an edited transcript of the proceedings, organised under the main headings of relevance to the media's performance before, and during the war respectively.

Before that, a summary of the main Reporting the World observations about the coverage, and recommendations for changes in covering future conflicts.

Observations

In many respects, coverage of the Iraq story was of a noticeably higher standard in UK media than that seen in previous wars.

Some journalists did expose misinformation and misrepresentations in the case for war after both Operation Desert Storm in 1991 and Operation Allied Force, the Nato bombing of Kosovo, in 1999. But, on those occasions, pursuing such angles remained a minority media pursuit. In this case, they were kept firmly on the agenda as a matter of vital public interest.

UK readers and audiences were much more likely, in this war, to be alerted to the possibility that claims from the proponents of war might be propaganda, or at least that information might be being presented in the service of a clearly identified agenda, and should be judged as such. There was a much greater 'meta-discussion' than in previous wars.

There were other significant changes, too. *Guardian* editor Alan Rusbridger drew attention to new difficulties, for governments intent on war and their propagandists, with the 'dehumanisation and demonisation' of the 'Other', which has remained an essential aspect of war propaganda.

That became much harder to do, he said, because of distinguished reporting on the people of Baghdad, their hopes and fears, by correspondents such as the *Guardian*'s own Suzanne Goldenberg and three participants in this discussion – Lindsey Hilsum of *Channel Four News*, Anton Antonowicz of the *Mirror* and David Chater of Sky News.

The Iraqi threat – were readers and audiences misled? How?

The main concern of many participants was the glaring discrepancy between the impression given of the threat from Iraq's weapons of mass destruction in coverage before the war; and the evidence available afterwards.

After the fall of Saddam Hussein, this issue continued to be picked over at great length in coverage of the UK Government's intelligence dossiers – presented as evidence from which the rationale for invading Iraq could be deduced but perhaps deployed as post-hoc justification for a decision already made.

The issues for journalists can be illustrated by examining some of the claims made, before the war, about the supposed threat from Iraq's 'weapons of mass destruction', and the way it was handled in the news.

One story was the allegation that a 'deadly drone' aircraft could be loaded with anthrax spores to menace global security; another concerned the demand that Iraq account for 10,000 litres of anthrax from 1991 to prove it was co-operating with UN weapons inspectors.

The fatal flaw in most coverage of such lines was that they tended to be repeated far more often than they were assessed or examined. (The figure, 'Anthrax – 10,000 litres' found its way into lots of television graphics, for instance, as was perhaps part of the intention).

This was one of the less credible claims because if, as 'litres' implies, the allegation was that Iraq had kept anthrax in liquid form, then, as any biochemist could have said, it would have had a shelf life of a couple of years at the most, i.e. it could not still be a threat twelve years later.

The drone story should have rung alarm bells because of the steady dripfeed of 'germ weapon threat' stories over the years, almost always attributed to nameless intelligence sources, which centred on drone aircraft. Any of these stories could have been knocked down with one simple fact – the range of the aircraft in question. In the mid-1990s, the talk was of a slightly more sophisticated version, an M-18 Dromeda, capable of flying some 300 miles or so. It meant that if, for instance, stories about threats to New York or Sydney were to stand up, the aircraft would have to be refuelled around 20 times en route from Iraq.

In the discussion, Lindsey Hilsum, stationed in Baghdad for *Channel Four News*, recalled that this, above all other claims about the supposed Iraqi threat, revealed to her 'the extent to which we were being sold a pup'.

Recommendation

Do not report a 'line' from an official source without obtaining and citing independent evidence as to its likely reliability. If, once evidence has been obtained, the reliability seems questionable, STOP repeating the line, or, if you do repeat it, always remind readers or audiences that independent evidence casts doubt on it.

It might have been as well, in this case, to remind readers and audiences from time to time of specifics about the history of dubious claims of an imminent threat from Iraqi chemical or biological weapons; and to make provision to hear from experts on the question of whether Iraq could have projected them, in this way, beyond its own borders.

Enabling debate

Did we do a good job of equipping readers and audiences to form their own views on the merits – or otherwise – of attacking Iraq?

This is where the coverage could have benefited from a much more innovative and creative approach, particularly during the period – bracketed, roughly, by the big demonstrations of 15 February and the invasion itself – when the debate was arguably at its most relevant.

The BBC's *War Guidelines*, issued in January 2003, describe concisely a task many journalists – both from the corporation and elsewhere – would recognise as a core function. Journalists should 'enable the national and international debate', they say, by 'allow[ing] the arguments to be heard and tested'. They continue: 'all views should be reflected to mirror the depth and spread of opinion'.

Key arguments in favour of war on Iraq boiled down to five essential propositions:

1. The crisis – later, the war – is really 'about' WMD
2. These pose an authentic threat to regional and world security
3. The only way to rid the world of this threat is regime change
4. Regime change is the only way to alleviate the grim humanitarian situation in Iraq
5. The only way to bring about regime change is war.

Of these, the second took centre stage after the war, and, by the time of this discussion, had raised the question uppermost by then in participants' minds – why was it not interrogated more effectively beforehand?

Before the war, the only one of these propositions really put to the test was the third. Crucially, the Franco-German call for the inspectors to be given more time offered an alternative, allowing readers and audiences to juxtapose what they were hearing from the US and UK governments with a countervailing proposition, and weigh them in the balance.

In all the other areas, countervailing propositions attracted little or no coverage. In the first, a large cross-section of the UK public believed all along that the crisis was not, or not primarily, 'about' WMD at all, but about a US agenda to install and maintain compliant governments in the world's main oil-producing region.

In a survey for Channel Four, which presented respondents with a menu of possible explanations, the 'security threat' topped the poll, with 22 per cent; but only by a narrow margin from the most popular alternative view. Fully 21 per cent told pollsters they thought it was really all about oil.

A second poll, for the Pew Research Center, setting up the question in a different way, found the oil theory was shared by fully 44 per cent of the British, and large majorities in many other countries.

Far from being 'reflected to mirror the depth and spread of opinion', however, this was almost entirely absent as an analytical factor in coverage of the build-up to war.

Likewise, with propositions four and five, there were plenty of ideas circulating for bringing about regime change without war (learning from the process which eventually brought down the iron curtain) and for improving the human rights situation of Iraqi people – but these, too were largely excluded.

Why were these perspectives, on three out of the five key arguments for war, so conspicuously missing from most coverage? At least partly because countervailing propositions, in these areas, were being put forward by what one participant, BBC World Service Europe region editor Bill Hayton, called 'non-traditional sources'.

Recommendation

Acknowledge that the important job of testing arguments is best done if they are juxtaposed with, and weighed against, alternative, countervailing arguments. If these do not issue from traditional sources, be on the lookout for opportunities to explore them by going to non-traditional sources.

News management

A fascinating input from Mary Dejevsky, diplomatic correspondent and foreign leader-writer on the *Independent*, highlighted the use of the Parliamentary Lobby in news management.

Key security stories, including the September dossier on Iraq's weapons, were handed out to Political Correspondents – bypassing specialist reporters who might have polluted them by raising, at the outset, some difficult questions.

Dejevsky drew rueful chuckles of recognition from participants when she described herself as 'the proud possessor of a denunciation email from John

Williams at the Foreign Office who accused me of "consistent negative coverage" and how I need to call up more frequently to "check the line" with the Foreign Office, as a lot of my colleagues do.'

This well-known technique of news management rests on a symbiotic relationship within the Westminster village. Compliant reporters get a steady dripfeed of exclusive stories from official sources; spin-doctors get a reliable conduit for their message to enter the public realm on favourable terms. But it proved, in this story, a major obstacle in the task of conveying a proper understanding to readers and audiences.

The effect is exacerbated by television news – particularly 24-hour news – in which a set-piece speech, statement or press conference by a senior politician is automatically treated as 'news' – regardless of whether what is being said addresses, or evades, the important questions.

Recommendation

All newsrooms genuinely interested in offering a service to the public must think long and hard about 'conduit' journalism and, in particular, whether their Political Correspondents are being used in this way. In covering speeches, statements or news conferences by politicians, precautions should be taken in advance to have reporters and commentators standing by, ready to point out omissions from what is being said, or elisions of key questions. They should not just be put on television automatically as an 'update'.

The discussion

Before the war
Why were the holes and discrepancies in the Government's case on Weapons of Mass Destruction not exposed before the war?

> **Ed Pilkington – Home News Editor, the *Guardian*** (Foreign Editor during the war)
> The weird thing about this war, and uniquely in my experience, is that the war itself is becoming increasingly a sideshow. The talk about embedding and talk about Basra, talk about Umm Qasr and all that – it is becoming increasingly marginal to the main question of how did we allow Tony Blair to get away with telling us that he had his own special intelligence and we must trust him? And he knew the truth? And we now know that he didn't have his own special intelligence and in fact virtually the entire lot of it was at least four years old and pre-1998, and we let him get away with that.

> **Mark Brayne – BBC Trauma Unit and Director, DART Centre Europe**
> I am fascinated by the psychology of what is happening with self-delusion. To explain

it extremely briefly ... we each of us have what psychologists call a 'schema' inside ourselves, which is a kind of roadmap of how the world works. When something challenges us that doesn't fit that schema, we can do one of two things. We can change our internal schema and adapt and say, 'oh well I was wrong,' and we move forward to the next level of understanding and awareness or we can say 'I am right,' how are we going to adjust the external schema and continue to search for evidence that I was right in the first place. I think we can draw conclusions from that about what is going on at levels of manipulation of information.

Kim Sengupta – the *Independent*

I think there was a view that anything the Iraqis said or did was not to be believed and that the US and Britain basically told the truth. I remember being in Baghdad and watching a Pentagon press conference on television, when Donald Rumsfeld talked about how the Iraqis were flouting the UN by firing at American and British aircraft in the no-fly zone.

Now, we all know the no-fly zones were not set up by the UN, they were set up by the US and Britain and France, they were nothing to do with the UN in that sense. But not one single reporter in that Pentagon press conference raised that question. Now, with huge apologies to our American friends here, someone said ah, well, that's the American press for you.

Then, when I got back to London in November, I remember Jack Straw said the same thing, and again, no one actually said no, it's nothing to do with the UN, it is an illegal no fly zone set up by America, so the Iraqis under international law had the right to fire back. I think to a certain extent what is happening now is because we were intrinsically less than critical enough at the time.

Lindsey Hilsum – Diplomatic correspondent, *Channel Four News*

[In Baghdad] we only really understood the extent to which we were being sold a pup a few days before the war when the Americans suddenly got very excited about a drone, which they said the weapons inspectors had hidden in their report but this drone was a terrible threat to the future of the world.

Now, the drone was like something out of *Aeromodellers Monthly*, it was made out of the fuselage of an aircraft, it was done up with duct tape and it had an engine which, as one American reporter put it, 'was smaller than a weed-whacker', which I gather is even smaller than a lawn mower, and we were told the Iraqis had hidden this programme.

We actually had pictures from the November trade fair where they were trying to sell these drones to other Arab countries and they were painted fluorescent pink, so that people would notice them. Now the Americans were telling us that this drone was a threat to the security of the world and it was only when we got to that point that we felt bold enough to say, 'hang on – I don't think so'.

Richard Sambrook – BBC Head of News

Well I think that hindsight is a fantastic thing, and clearly we've been through the developments of the last few weeks wishing perhaps we had raised some of these questions last autumn or in the early part of this year and tried to sort them out then, but we didn't. On the threat, we probably didn't for the reason that we were not able to pursue it at that stage, and I'm glad that we haven't let it go and that we're still pursuing it.

Alan Rusbridger – Editor, the *Guardian*

We had the same difficulty as the BBC over sources. We were hearing a lot of the same stuff as Richard was but it was coming out through necessarily anonymous sources and that makes the whole business of securing stuff precisely very difficult. So I think that process will go on and on and on and take many months, if not years to peel back.

Andy McLean – Saferworld

One interesting question for me is why did Niger not make a bigger story earlier on? Because, before the war, the IAEA said these are forged documents and so on, and it got some coverage but didn't really get picked up. I remember wondering, why were more people not running with this?

Mary Dejevksy – Diplomatic Correspondent, the *Independent*

It wasn't picked up because chemical and biological weapons trumped it and because the IAEA said we don't believe they have nuclear weapons – so nuclear weapons were basically off the agenda – what was on the agenda was chemical and biological. Now the chemical and biological weapons have gone, at least for the moment – that is why the nuclear thing has come back.

Was the anti-war case given fair coverage?

Bill Hayton – Europe Region Editor, BBC World Service

We obviously covered the big demonstration [on 15 February] in a fair and proper way but we should have reached out more to dig out these voices of dissent.

The stuff that was going on in [RAF] Fairford [the air base from which US B52 bombers took off to bomb Iraq] was staggering. The bombs were on one side of the road and they had to be taken across a public highway into the airfield and they were being driven along at five miles an hour and people would chain themselves on and bomb vehicles that kept moving with people chained to them, this is a fantastic story but we didn't cover it.

There was a protest where people went out in buses from London, they were held at a road block several miles from Fairford for a couple of hours, then turned around and bundled off. They would have been arrested if they didn't, there was a police escort on all four sides of the coaches. People on the buses rang the BBC newsroom and were told they were lying this couldn't possibly be happening. These stories were not getting on because we weren't reaching out to these protestors and these non-traditional voices to get them in.

Jake Lynch – Co-Director, Reporting the World

The BBC's *War Guidelines* say 'all views should be reflected to mirror the depth and spread of opinion', which is a very useful phrase and honoured perhaps in some cases more in the breach than the observance. They also call for the arguments to be 'heard and tested'.

Just briefly to review the main arguments in favour of the war: firstly the crisis, later the war is really about Iraq's weapons of mass destruction and threat they pose to global security; secondly, the only way to remove or neutralise that threat is by regime change; the third was the only way to achieve regime change is war and fourth, which was kind of made up along the way, was that war would therefore do most to improve the humanitarian situation for the Iraqi people.

Now, I would suggest that of those four the only one that was really tested was the second, because it could be juxtaposed with an alternative proposition, the French, German and later Russian position that no, the only way to neutralise that threat is not by regime change but also by letting the inspectors continue their work.

So personally, I think the lesson from the reporting of this conflict might be that we need to look harder and cast our net wider for alternative propositions to set alongside the propositions being given to us in the grid, the Downing Street grid, the White House grid or the Pentagon grid of daily developments, because otherwise they will be lost beneath the daily deluge of troop deployments, dossiers, press briefings, diplomatic shuttles, etc, etc, which can obscure questions that we started with.

Richard Sambrook – BBC Head of News

I think the period before the war was very peculiar. In a sense you have two discussions, one about the pre-conflict period and then about the conflict itself, and for the BBC the pre-conflict period was very difficult for us because it was the first time, certainly in my professional life, that Britain has gone to war with the country so deeply divided, so how do you achieve some impartiality and some fairness?

David Seymour – Group Political Editor, the *Mirror*

What in fact happened was that – it was partly a feeling in the office, and partly getting some sort of feedback – it wasn't that we were particularly pro or anti – although obviously we were anti – but that the paper was unremittingly negative and the sort of stories like the rescue of (Private) Lynch were the odd – untrue as it may be – were the odd positive thing to come through.

If you remember, I think by the second week, all the papers, even the pro-war papers, we were all consistent in saying the thing is going completely wrong. Rumsfeld has only sent a half or a quarter of the number of troops he should have sent in there and it is all going wrong. We looked at the paper, and you would have had one of Anton [Antonowicz]'s great reports [from Baghdad] in there but it would be, from a British perspective, negative – we were killing civilians, Americans were killing civilians and then you see somebody else killed, and then you see something going wrong somewhere else, and that was the stage where you were trying to say well do you really want to do that? Is what you are doing to your readers so depressing them?

Alan Rusbridger – Editor, the *Guardian*

In every war you try and depersonalise the enemy and dehumanise them but I think having someone of Suzanne Goldenberg's quality inside Baghdad talking to ordinary Iraqis and making them terribly human is a new element in war, and you can see why politicians don't like it but it also makes it extremely difficult to go to war on a nation when you are getting that kind of image and I think the humanity of her reporting and Lindsey's (Hilsum, *Channel Four News*) was just of a different calibre and texture from the reporting we'd seen before and that will in some way make fundamental changes in how war is seen.

How was the news managed on the 'home front'?

Mary Dejevsky – Diplomatic Correspondent, the *Independent*

The two dossiers which have now become so much the topic of debate were not presented to us, the diplomatic correspondents who might have been expected to be given the dossiers for perusal first.

The first one was released to the lobby, which became a practice, and the second one was released I gather at 7am in the morning to correspondents for the Sunday newspapers covering a trip to the US. So we were basically cut out of the loop. And there was that feeling the whole time that anybody who had sort of specialist expertise or experience in London in the Whitehall operation was deliberately given second class treatment.

The second problem with covering the Foreign Office was that you were continually trumped by the Lobby, that the briefings that the Foreign Office conducted basically duplicated what the Lobby had been given and you had to compare notes to pick up what was going on.

I now think, with the benefit of hindsight, that a lot of people at the Foreign Office were very unhappy at the sort of stuff that they were feeding us. I was certainly extremely unhappy with the stuff the Foreign Office was feeding us, including the two dossiers, and the spin that the Foreign Office was putting on it, to the point where I am the proud possessor of a denunciation email from John Williams at the Foreign Office who accused me of 'consistent negative coverage', and how I need to call up more frequently to 'check the line' with the Foreign Office as a lot of my colleagues do ...

I would just like to make two points about the dossiers. I think we probably all do a lot of breastbeating in retrospect as to why didn't we challenge them, well from somebody who did challenge them to the Foreign Office, the context was very different, because then there was always the risk that, the very next day, they were going to find piles of the stuff all over Iraq in the very places where they said would do, so you were at a great disadvantage expressing the scepticism that I was doing. It was a high-risk thing to do and it was also very difficult for editors, because they were very reluctant to pursue that line as a reporting line. They were happy to pursue it in editorials, columns – fine.

During the war

Did we manage to sift propaganda from fact?

Tony Maddox – Senior Vice President of CNN International
I think what was difficult, for 24 hour news specifically, was that this was one of those stories where there were lots of sources of information that were very difficult to check and you were in the process of having to say, well do we sit on this until we check it out, in which case others are going to run with it and we'll get the blame if it proves to be true, or alternatively we pump it out there and we reserve the right to pull it back afterwards. So there was quite a bit of that balancing act going on and no-one got away clean on that, we were all caught up in this.

[On] the point about Basra and Umm Qasr and the different reports which were based on reasonable sourcing at the time – as the conflict went on we became, all of us, more savvy about what we were broadcasting and I think it is certainly true to say that if I had my time over again there are certain stories we would have sat on and certain stories we would have gone to air with more quickly.

Richard Sambrook – BBC Head of News
You get a better flavour but you are now further up the information chain in the field, so that is why you get the news like Umm Qasr has fallen and there's an uprising in Basra, because you are hearing from the military before they have worked out what is happening and you are live on air telling the world about it before they really know what is going on.

That's compounded by the nature of 24 hour broadcasting, where the audience are alongside you trying to work out what is happening, and even if we think we can understand the issues it raises, I am quite sure the audience doesn't, which is why you got people saying, 'the BBC says this and it turns out to be wrong'. Well, what we said was what we thought we'd been told at the time, and if it then turned out to be wrong we had to go back and correct it.

John Kampfner, Political Editor, *New Statesman* and reporter on the BBC Correspondent film, *War Spin*

We focused mostly on the Jessica Lynch story [for the film] and … we were wilfully misinterpreted by the Pentagon. They suggested that we were saying that the Americans should not have gone in heavily armed, with reinforcements, into Nasiriyah, into the hospital to seize her. After all, the idea that the Fedayeen had gone, they'd been told it, they were right not necessarily to trust it.

No, the issue – as the Iraqi doctors told us in our film – was the way it was spun by the Americans afterwards, turning what was a pretty professional and heavy operation into a heroic operation. What they needed to have said afterwards was, yes, we went into there all guns blazing, we were right to do that; however, we could have simply opened the door of the hospital and walked in, and the doctors were there, there was no military there, ready to hand her over, in fact they wanted to hand her over a couple of days earlier in an ambulance, but the Americans started firing at the ambulance, so they had to go back. So it's interesting to see the Americans [now] basically resiling from all their criticism.

Bill Hayton – Europe Region Editor, BBC World Service

The story that the Iraqis had fired Scuds – if they had fired Scuds that is a prima facie case that they were in breach of UN resolutions. Now it may have been a military spokesman that said it but I'm afraid we repeated it unchallenged, we didn't say missiles, we said Scuds, it went round too long in my view.

Was it possible to report properly from Baghdad?

Lindsey Hilsum – Diplomatic Correspondent, *Channel Four News*

There were complicated decisions every day on how far to push it. You are not supposed to go out by yourself, you're supposed to only go out on the Saga Tours holiday bus, which takes you on a rubble tour. Now at what point do you not do that and say 'bugger it, I need to go out and talk to people', and we all made different decisions, crept out and talked to people with or without camera and so on. Looking back I wish I had done more than that but in the end we survived and we got out as accurate a picture as we could.

I think one of the important things that we did which we could do was to reflect to some extent what Iraqi people thought and felt. We could not obviously report a lot of what Iraqi people said to us. Some Iraqis talked to me about what they felt about Saddam Hussein, about the regime. I remember one student who came up to me and said, 'we want this war, we want change'. Nothing in the world would have made me report that because that young man could be dead now if I had done. We have all been criticised for censoring ourselves, but I am glad I don't have the death of this young man on my conscience, what can you do?

But I think other Iraqis were able to be honest to us about what it felt like to be under bombing and missile attacks and the insecurity they felt and I think that as the war progressed and it was clear that Iraqi Government was losing, we were able to report more and more what people really said to us.

Kim Sengupta – the *Independent*
There was self-censorship for pretty laudable reasons. I've also got to say before the war there was also self-censorship for purely selfish reasons. We wanted that all-important golden visa, we wanted to not upset people too much, and to that extent self-censorship went on and I am pretty much as guilty as anyone else on that.

Anton Antonowicz – Chief Feature Writer, the *Mirror*
Just briefly back to Baghdad and embeds, I can't help but think that all of us in Baghdad were in fact embedded, in fact we were being held in a kind of custody by fairly horrible people who wanted to show us very horrible things for their own even more ghastly motives, but actually it was quite easy in Baghdad, because you would just follow the script. The opportunities for being analytical on the ground were very very few. What one could do in the end was come out with little more, I suspect, than the Christmas cracker platitude that war is a horrible thing and innocent people get killed.

Was it possible to report properly from embedded positions with US and UK forward units?

Air Marshal Sir Tim Garden – Centre for Defence Studies, King's College, London and former Assistant Chief of Defence Staff
The embedded bit seemed to me to be done pretty well by those who were there, but you have to remember that that actually determines what the news agenda is and actually there were lots of important things that were not covered by embedded journalists – special forces operations, what was going on in the western desert and what is probably, when you look at the endgame of all of this, the thing that determined the way the war was shaped – that was the full air task order activity, which isn't sort of the embedded bit, and the failure, from my point of view, was not the journalists' failure but was an extraordinary failure in the Centcom Headquarters, which was appalling.

Richard Sambrook – BBC Head of News
After Kosovo Jamie Shea did a speech in Bosnia where he basically said that their frustration had been that it didn't matter whatever happened, if there were pictures of a civilian tractor being hit that became the narrative of the day. And I think the embedded policy came out of that because he said they would have to grab the

pictures of the day to grab the narrative. I wonder whether we reflected on that when actually we had no pictures of the Republican Guard, we had no pictures of the western desert – was embedding simply a means of capturing the narrative of the day in a controlled way.

Phillip Knightley – journalist, and author of *The First Casualty*
The embedded idea rose partly out the fact that in the war against the former Yugoslavia NATO succeeded in winning that war without the loss of a single Nato military person for the first time in the history of war. And the military looked around and said wait a minute, if there were no military heroes to talk about, that explains why all the journalists focused on the human interest stories and the victims, bad for the military! We don't want them writing stories about people being bombed and shot and murdered, so this time we are going get over that by embedding the correspondents with the military so that all they can write about is the activities of the troops that they are embedded with.

What are we going to do with the next war? Are we going to go along with the embedded idea? The main danger I can see with that is not so much that you'll be limited to the group that you are with but the psychological identification that grows between the embedded correspondent and the soldiers he is with, the use of the 'we', 'we're doing this, and we're doing that'. And it was frankly admitted by one BBC correspondent that he got involved in the action because the soldiers around him said, 'what are you doing here? Help us!' so he helped them.

Audrey Gillan – Reporter, the *Guardian* (embedded with the Household Cavalry)
We have to acknowledge that being embedded has its limitations because you do not have very much freedom of movement, ability to go off and interview who you like. We have no translators with us, basically no control, we're seeing what they want us to see, although in my experience it wasn't that they could control what I saw because I was there with them, a frontline fighting unit, so they couldn't say you can't come here or there because I was actually with them.

Censorship was an issue, for some of these discussions I have been involved in; it has not been so much of an issue for other people but certainly I know a lot of journalists who were censored; I was censored, sometimes quite rightly where I was in breach of security and could have brought us into great danger. Other issues were simply stylistic, things like 'running for cover' was changed to 'dashing for cover' because running for cover implies cowardice.

Certain elements of what was perceived to be anti-Americanism was removed and Ed (Pilkington), who was the Foreign Editor of the *Guardian* at the time, had asked me to do this piece about the situation we were talking about, about boredom. We were in the desert for a couple of days, not knowing what the hell was going on and what we were going to do. I went out and spoke to all the guys and they were like, 'well this is just rubbish'. And basically I had to cut back lots of it, because they said, 'we'll all get sent home if you run that. We can't say that the whole unit is really fucked off'.

Andrew North – BBC Radio Reporter

I was with the US Marines, which was very different because there was no censorship for me at all. I was live on air, sometimes up to forty times a day, and no-one was checking what I was doing once we crossed over. I had to get permission before we crossed over the line, to go live, but after that I just reported whatever was happening.

What the Americans saw they would get out of it was that by having so many journalists out there they knew that everyone would be desperate to get on air to get their particular bit of action, it did generate a lot of drama and then as a result of that you did forget about the big picture, there was so much of this stuff coming through.

Yet at the same time we did get information. Given what was going on at Centcom – Centcom were not giving anything. The embeds, and I've heard this from so many different editors, the stuff we were providing on the ground was the only information they were getting.

Were western media too squeamish in not showing the gory effects of war?

Lindsey Hilsum, Diplomatic Correspondent, Channel Four News

When I was young we used to bang on about this thing called, 'the New World Information Order' which was going to be imposed by UNESCO, it has in fact been created by technology. There were two Indian TV stations there [in Baghdad], there was a Bangladeshi reporter for a newspaper, Philippines television was there, everybody was in Baghdad. The rest of the world was not depending on European and American broadcasters and newspapers anymore, so that is a real change, something new and very important.

Phillip Knightley – journalist, and author of *The First Casualty*

The ending of the western monopoly of television reporting, the arrival on the scene of *Al Jazeera* and Arab TV, are going to change the nature of what the western reporters have to do.

And there'll be more gratuitous violence I am afraid because the whole point of Arab TV is going to be to show victims, they'll be victim correspondents, victim correspondents seen on the scene, gratuitous violence, the real face of battle is going to force western TV networks to consider whether they too can continue to ignore what war is all about.

Richard Sambrook, BBC Head of News

The pictures issue is a narrow one, it is easy to say we need to show the horror of war for people to understand it, I think that is too easy and cheap an argument, we have responsibility as broadcasters for what we are putting into people's living rooms with families watching. Having said that I think we got it wrong this time. You have to decide where you draw the line, we were probably too conservative this time. We need to look very hard at that, but it's wrong to think you can just pump out pictures of carnage.

Were US media concerned with telling, or selling?

Danny Schechter – Executive Editor, MediaChannel.org

We've had a divided country at least since November 2000, probably before, the red states and the blue states, the Gore versus Bush people; the large unprecedented anti-war movement, which materialised in the US and grew alongside movements in other parts of the world, led to the feeling on the part of a lot of people who were active, that they were electronically disenfranchised, that their voice was not showing up on American television, that their voices were not being included for the most part in the American media; and there are studies analysing the guests on television shows, how many took what positions, and you see a process of marginalisation of voices who are critical of the Administration.

We also have the Fox effect, which is a very significant effect of a news channel that was taking a political stance and packaging it as fair and balanced journalism, real journalism even, and aggressively going after journalists it didn't like, who were critical in any way or perceived to be critical. Peter Arnett for example was targetted by Fox news, which was one of the reasons that MSNBC responded.

MSNBC set out to transform its programme schedule to out-Fox Fox as they put it, and the head of the channel said they were up against the 'patriotism police' – people who were actually monitoring MSNBC coverage – and so they moved to the position of putting promos on the air that said, 'God bless America'; 'let freedom reign' and the rest of it. So we had a wave of patriotic correctness.

… I've tried to argue that essentially that there were three media wars going on.

The war that you saw in Europe, the war that people saw in the Middle East and the war that we saw in America and the different wars with different focus and a different emphasis … I challenge this notion that was very common in the media heads of power, that we can't get ahead of our audience, the audience was gung-ho for the war, therefore we have to give the audience what it wants, and I think in doing so there was an abdication of journalistic responsibility.

Tony Maddox – Senior Vice President of CNN International

The point you make Danny is a very fair one, many people who have seen CNN-USA saw it criticise the robustness of the challenges that were being made to the US government. The fact is CNN-USA went a lot further than most of the other US networks in what it did and still finds itself now being derided as unpatriotic, leftwing, too Democratic, because there is a spirit of intolerance which I perceive as a Brit when

I visit the US and talk to my American colleagues, a spirit of intolerance which seems to have got inculcated beyond Fox.

People talk about Fox a lot. Fox are a cable channel like we are, on a day to day basis they only have a limited amount of appeal but its effect seems to me to have run much wider and certainly don't discount the effect of talk radio which is enormously well listened to and has quite a right-wing agenda, so there is this idea that anyone who is not for us is against us, and they created this zero-sum game which is actually quite widespread.

Now if you watch NBC, CBS, ABC or CNN. I suspect I probably saw more of that than most people in this room. The fact is, there was some very good reporting took place by some very talented journalists who were asking quite probing questions.

Lindsey Hilsum – Diplomatic Correspondent, *Channel Four News*

I'm going to stick up for some of the American print media – in Baghdad there was a real contrast, because when the America broadcasters and TV all pulled out ostensibly on safety grounds – I suspect also on grounds that they had been pressured and partly the Pentagon told them they would be killed because it wasn't safe – and the MoD told British broadcasters the same, the British broadcasters stood firm and the America newspapers were also all there.

The *New York Times* was there, the *Washington Post* had two correspondents – even a paper as small as the *Atlanta Constitution* had two correspondents there, the *Sacramento* Bee was there, so I do think that American newspapers did extremely well in staying in Baghdad and reporting daily.

Did the US military deliberately set out to make life impossible for journalists to report from any but embedded positions?

David Chater – Senior Correspondent, Sky News based in Baghdad

I think [embedding] is a serious abdication of journalistic responsibility, I am not used to it as a war reporter, I am used to being unilateral and making my own decisions.

I am not trying to take away from those who are embedded but theirs was a very restricted view, but it was a very vivid view and the TV technology was there to put it across to people and that is one of main dangers I think – that there were 1,200 unilateral journalists operating outside that system, and they had a very, very hard time.

The Americans especially gave them a very hard time. It was very dangerous for them, they took a lot of casualties, but on top of that we were using technology now which we are going to use increasingly in warfare to bring the very frontline straight into people's living rooms live and that is a very dangerous development for the journalist.

Richard Sambrook, BBC Head of News

[Operating unilaterally] was more difficult than in any conflict in the last few years, certainly on safety grounds. We were inhibited from being able to work independently to the extent that we would have liked, and that definitely had an impact on the journalism on the overview we were able to present.

Tony Maddox – Senior Vice President of CNN International

The death toll amongst the journalistic community was, and continues to be, quite disgraceful. It's appalling, the amount of casualties, I mean the group that went out there, we probably, as a battalion of journalists, suffered as many losses as anybody. And I think as editors that is still something that we are coming to terms with.

Phillip Knightley – journalist, and author of *The First Casualty*

It is an undisputed fact that fifteen journalists died in this war, more than in any other war with such duration in history. To put it in perspective, in the second World War BBC reporters covered the war in Europe from the time of the Normandy invasion until the surrender of Germany, and lost only two reporters. Fifteen lost in less than a month is a disgraceful state of affairs.

And we have to remind ourselves that the largest single group of those were killed by American fire. Accident? Design? I don't know but I think the American Government is now adopting the attitude towards unilaterals which is simply this: 'we think it intolerable that any red-blooded American or any coalition journalist should want to report the war with the enemy side and if they do and they get in our way we will fire at them.' I can't prove that but I think that is a very, very likely scenario.

Broadcasting and government panic in the Iraq crisis

Ros Brunt

How was the media discussed in the UK during the Iraq crisis of 2003? An 'accusatory mode' of political and analytical debate denounced the media for lies, bias and collusion with government propaganda. This article offers a different perspective that highlights some of the contradictions and 'leakiness' in broadcast coverage. It looks at the UK government's own hostility to the mainstream media coverage of Iraq and its attack on the BBC for having a biased 'anti-war agenda'. The Hutton enquiry and report demonstrated the BBC responding to a variety of views about the Iraq war and insisting on the legitimacy of anti-war opinions.

In this article I want to consider how discussion in Britain around the Iraq crisis tended to be dominated by accusations against the media. Whether it was in classroom debate or during anti-war protest on the streets, I was struck by how easily a vocabulary of lies, propaganda and deliberate misinformation was repeatedly invoked against the media. I want first to unpick how this 'accusatory' approach worked and then go on to outline some of the implications of adopting a different approach that starts by taking the media 'seriously' in their own terms and looks at what media organisations and practitioners themselves say about what they do. The media examples I'll take will be from British broadcasting at different points of 2003 and from the government investigation started in the summer of that year and known as the Hutton Enquiry, whose primary context was indeed allegations of 'bias' and 'lying' against the BBC – originating in this case, however, not from anti-war campaigners or students of media studies, but from the instigators of the war themselves, the UK Labour Government.

First, by referring to an 'accusatory' approach, I mean one that assumes that an undifferentiated and monopolistic media system is at work, where 'the media' always operates in the singular. The usage that claims 'the media is …' is so widespread now it's pedantic to make a grammatical objection. But as a teacher I do still try to make the conceptual point that treating 'the media' as singular tends to encourage a unilinear perspective, a notion of an all-encompassing homogeneous and unchanging entity, which appears either 'too' or 'all' powerful to its accusers. Their next step is then to assume that this singular entity works in close conjunction with another monolith, 'the' state or 'the' government, in ways that inevitably and obviously produce propaganda, bias or lies. However, such accusations do not implicate the accusers themselves in any media contamination for they have access to other forms of knowledge that enable them to 'see through' the duping and doping that's being perpetrated on the mainstream media audience.

The accusatory mode concerns me because it lacks both analytical and political effectivity. When I hear it in the classroom it often replaces the rigour and subtlety required for any adequate analytical critique of the media with a passionate, but ultimately reductive, pursuit of catching the media out in collusion with the state. And when it emanates from a dissenting anti-war platform, whilst it comes across as a powerful media-savvy, don't-mess-with-us position, it is the product of a kind of knowingness that knows little but cynicism and actually implies a weakness and powerlessness in confronting 'the media-state onslaught'. For if no real differentiation can be made between various media and if 'the media' can be so glibly elided with state interests, then that becomes the end of the matter. When 'the media' is repeatedly invoked and evoked as merely an unproblematic ally of state, a version of politics emerges which has no time for complexity or contradiction and hence leaves no room for any worthwhile political intervention that might engage with the strategies, practices and content of different media: political answers become predictable and inevitable and any further analysis is inhibited. This is a politics that makes for defeatism and quietist resignation, despite its often vehement rhetoric. Just as it overestimates the unilateral force of the media-state connection, so it simultaneously underestimates any political possibilities 'on the ground' of civil society, such as, indeed, marches and demonstrations, and their potential impact on media coverage.

Both political and analytical forms of the accusatory mode feature in the first collection of articles to appear on the media's role in Iraq: *Tell Me Lies: Propaganda and Media Distortion in the Attack on Iraq.*[1] Its polemical title not only makes direct reference to Adrian Mitchell's poem about media and state propaganda during the war in Vietnam, but is also indicative of the approach taken by its authors – British and American academics, journalists and political commentators. For whilst they are careful to interpret the UK and US media as plural, a vocabulary of bias is employed as if all its terms – *propaganda, lies, distortion, misinformation, disinformation, inaccuracy, legitimation* … – amount to equivalent, interchangeable accusations. So it becomes unimportant to discern which element of this biased coverage might be deliberate; or to consider whether, say, propaganda, should be distinguished from inaccuracy. Such distinctions don't really count for much because the essential end-point of most of the book's articles is to prove once more what the authors already knew from the off: that the media are inevitably biased towards the status quo and hence systematically undermine dissent.

When I first read *Tell Me Lies* I was looking through a spate of current affairs programmes which had appeared on mainstream British TV channels in September and October 2003 – a period when the media appeared to 'catch up' with the aftermath of the Iraq war and, following the traditionally 'light' summer scheduling, offer their first, widely researched think-pieces on the situation. Examples of these were several documentaries on the dismal life chances of Iraqi children who had been mutilated by American weapons. These films were deliberately counterpointed with the *cause celèbre* of thirteen-year-old Ali Abbas who had lost both arms in a US missile attack and been airlifted to a UK hospital courtesy of the British tabloid press. They thus undermined any impression either that Ali Abbas had been the only child amputee of the war or that his expensive treatment might be at all typical. Then BBC 1's *Panorama* kicked off the autumn season with a highly sceptical examination of 'The Price of Victory' (28.09.03), based on three months' summer filming of American troops, civilians and policy makers in Baghdad. Meanwhile ITV and Channel 4 coverage of the war included documentaries from John Pilger, the veteran Australian journalist who first came to prominence with his exposé of the Cambodian 'killing fields', and Mark Thomas, the British political comedian and investigative journalist. Both Pilger and Thomas were key contributors to *Tell Me Lies*, and their articles in that collection had both endorsed and exemplified an accusatory approach to the media. But what interested me about their own broadcasting and journalism practice as demonstrated in these autumn programmes was how it told a quite different story: one that highlighted effective, well-researched and politically challenging uses of the mainstream media.

In the lead-up to the war, John Pilger had been investigating both Iraq and the continuing crisis in Afghanistan, with reports that dominated both tabloid and broadsheet journalism. His had been the star name exemplifying the consistently anti-war stance of *The Daily Mirror*. The paper's front pages had combined stark photojournalism with headlines like: '*BLOOD ON HIS HANDS – John Pilger: His most damning verdict on Tony Blair*', referring to a graphic picture of the prime minister caught, literally, red-handed, over the anti-war slogan 'NOT IN OUR NAME' (29.01.03). Now here was Pilger on ITV in September with a detailed hour-long investigation, *Breaking the Silence: Truth and Lies in the War on Terror* (22.09.03), employing characteristic punchy polemic and pointed argument from high-ranking global experts and local witnesses to examine the USA's role as 'the biggest terrorist in the world', with case-studies including Afghanistan, Chile, and Cambodia, as well as the Middle-East .

By contrast, Mark Thomas demonstrated his idiosyncratic style of spoof-but-serious reportage in C4's *Mark Thomas: Debt Collector* (22.10.03). In the programme, he adopted the punning conceit of 'alms for Iraq', to pursue arms manufacturers and other major American and British capitalists around various summer business and arms fairs in London, sweetly requesting reparations for the country that he most courteously hinted they were currently pillaging. He also politely invited them to justify their interest in Iraq – which several unwisely did – before he revealed the total they'd donated to his charity box: £34.

Now in scheduling terms, these programmes were quite marginalised, transmitted at the tail-end of evening viewing – a consequence of the loss of mainstream regular 'public service' current affairs programming in prime time, and its replacement with lifestyle and human interest documentaries plus the extended staples of series and serials. So if this is the current climate of consumption-led, competitive broadcasting, how come such a diverse and expensively-resourced range of programmes gets on the schedules? And further, if the mainstream media are as complicit with state propaganda as *Tell Me Lies* proposes, then the interesting question for me becomes: how could programmes that broadly dissent from, or at least substantially question, the UK government's policies on Iraq get commisioned in the first place?

It was considering how you'd begin to account for the very existence of such critique-ing programmes on air, even though not in prime time, that made me think about explanatory frameworks for analysing current affairs broadcasting. For explanatory frameworks are usually rendered redundant within an accusatory perspective. 'Findings' and 'results' are what count – with the stacking up of instances of lies, propaganda, etc., which are then followed by self-evident conclusions about state-media collusion.

So it might be useful to start where the accusatory mode usually ends. I would expect that mainstream broadcasting organisations, licensed and legislated for by the state, would generally tend *in some way* to reproduce and represent its political, social and economic realities. Whilst this approach would inform the starting point of an investigation into broadcast journalism, the *'in some way'* would always be crucial to the analysis, and media research would stay alert to the notion that the realities represented would not go uncontested. From this perspective, media coverage would thus never be seamlessly and unproblematically aligned with 'the interests of state' – which, themselves, might well be in a process of flux, transition and conflict.

This approach focuses the investigative interest on the element of surprise in media coverage. Instead of being on the look-out for repeated instances of the same-old-same-old broadcasting sins, it highlights the unpredictable moments. For instance, when the sources of a story cannot control how it's represented; when dissenting voices are heard; or when live, or even edited pictures offer contradictory and plural readings of events. For broadcasting systems, however tightly controlled and restricted, will always be, to resurrect the Enzensberger notion, in a state of *leakiness*.[2]

This is why I'm interested in reversing the question and starting at the point where the accusatory mode seems to drive to a full stop: instead of providing yet further evidence of lies, bias and propaganda, to place the emphasis on the surprising bits of leakiness, examining the provenance of contradictions in media coverage, looking at the content that doesn't immediately 'fit' and noting any of the smaller qualifications, the *ifs*, *buts* and *howevers* that ruffle the official versions of events.

Take one example of a big leaky television moment that managed to achieve maximum global impact just three days after the start of the war. The Annual Hollywood Academy Awards ceremony, scheduled for March 2003 was intended to be extra-special to celebrate its 75th anniversary. In view of impending war, there were proposals for cancelling or postponing it before the decision was made to go ahead but in a suitably dressed-down, reflecting-the-state-of-the-nation kind of way. So the stars arrived, solemn, unglitzy and mainly in unadorned black. When time came for the Best Documentary Feature award, it was won by the polemical journalist Michael Moore for *Bowling for Columbine* (2002), his Canadian-financed investigation of the US gun laws in the light of a recent high school massacre by teenage students. Following a standing ovation, this was Moore's acceptance speech:

> Ah – on behalf of our producers, Catherine Glen and Michael Dawson from Canada *(cheers)*, um, I'd like to thank the Academy for this *(applause)*.
>
> We like non-fiction. We like non-fiction and we live in fictitious times. We live in the time when we have fictitious results that elect a fictitious President *(boos begin, increasing as speech continues; scattered applause; reaction-shots register shock, embarrassment, faint smiles of assent from star audience members)*. We live in a time when we have a man sending us to war for fictitious reasons, whether it's the 'fiction' of duck tape or the 'fictions' of orange alerts *(MM shouting against audience noise)*. We are against this war, Mr Bush! Shame on you Mr Bush!
>
> *(MM flourishes Oscar; band strikes up)* And any time you've got the Pope *and* the Dixie Chicks[3] against you, your time is up! (BBC-1 23.03.03).

Michael Moore's speech demonstrated media leakiness in several ways. For a global audience it was at least a chink in the armour of American hegemony. Being a 'live' event intended to tell the world the US was carrying on more sombrely but 'as normal', it was thereby 'open' to disruption by a voice that was at once both dissenting and legitimately award-winning. From this position, Moore could hardly be silenced without denying the very 'free speech' that the free world was supposedly promoting in Bush's war of Good v. Evil.

When he described the contradictory 'leaky' nature of the media Enzensberger also drew attention to what he called 'the open secret of the electronic media'.

This he said was 'their mobilising power' and it constituted 'the decisive political factor' about the media. In a situation where the primary media mobilisation was the articulation of a nation united behind Bush, Moore's audacious use of the first person plural could begin to mobilise a constituency around a different way of thinking. Linking everyday experiences of what 'we' like and how 'we' live to a notion of 'us' being sent to war and a 'we' who are against the war – though as yet only an inchoate minority – was a way of articulating 'an imaginary community' of dissent. It could thus provide, not only an alternative perspective on the US for a global audience, but also appeal to otherwise fragmented and isolated American dissenters themselves.

Indeed, one of the immediate mobilising effects of Moore's speech was on American troops landing in Iraq. They began corresponding with Moore to say how he'd crystallised their own increasing dissatisfaction with America's war aims. With their permission, and acknowledging the disciplinary risks they were running, Moore began posting on his website extracts such as this from the troops' letters:

> Here's what Specialist Mike Prysner of the US Army wrote to me:
>
> 'Dear Mike, I'm writing this without knowing if it'll ever get to you … I'm writing it from the trenches of a war (that's still going on) not knowing why I'm here or when I'm leaving … I joined the army as soon as I was eligible, eager to serve my country … Two years later I found myself moments away from a landing onto a pitch black airstrip, ready to charge into a country I didn't believe I belonged in, your words (from the Oscars) repeating in my head. My time in Iraq has always involved finding things to convince myself that I can be proud of my actions; that I was a part of something just. But no matter what pro-war argument I came up with, I pictured my smirking commander-in-chief, thinking he was fooling a nation … '[4]

On the website Moore adds his own commentaries to the extracts, offering, for instance, an analysis of the class-divide between America's power elite and the predominantly working-class troops they've sent to war, whose main reasons for enlisting had been job-security and the chance of a college education. He then goes on to address Iraqi civilians and anti-war groups as well as the troops and their families with a list of campaigning measures for supporting each group both practically and politically.

But leaky moments may often have a much less obvious political effectivity and work on a much smaller scale. To change the metaphor, they may operate more like Gramsci's 'cracks and fissures' that have the potential, if reflected on, to chop up a bit of hegemony. I'm thinking here of minor qualifications and modifications that may be inserted into the larger current affairs picture.

One example comes from the television news coverage of the capture of Saddam

Hussein in December 2003. This was an unexpected 'breaking' news event in Britain, starting late morning on a Sunday, normally the slackest news time, with constant updates as news organisations scrambled to edit new and old information together. By the late evening main television bulletins it was quite clear what was emerging as the dominant news paradigm. All the mainstream broadcasting channels focused on a dramatic narrative of hubris, telling a graphically illustrated tale of how luxurious palaces and unrestricted power had, via American nemesis, come down to 'a hole in the ground' for Saddam Hussein and a degrading public medical examination. The use of footage exclusive to the American military underscored a primarily triumphalist agenda that appeared to vindicate, if only temporarily, the continuing presence of the occupying Coalition forces; pictures of Saddam's humiliation were repeatedly twinned with the earlier iconic image from April as the war neared its end: the pulling down of Saddam's statue in Baghdad.

All the broadcast bulletins about the capture included a resumé section about Saddam Hussein's life and BBC-1's began in similar style to the others with reference to the falling statue:

> *Newsreader, Huw Edwards*: There are, potentially, countless charges which could be detailed at a trial. Saddam ruled for over two decades. His regime was responsible for the deaths of thousands of Iraqis, including several members of Saddam's own family. Rageh Omaar, who reported from Baghdad during the conflict … has this assessment of Iraq's years under Saddam:
>
> *Rageh Omaar: (voice-over)* Eight long months ago, the world saw the vestiges of a feared and despised dictator torn down in Baghdad *(toppling statue)*. This was the moment his regime collapsed. But the man himself was still free and he haunted ordinary Iraqis who feared his return.
>
> Saddam Hussein reached into every home and street *(portraits, statues, posters)*. It made Iraqis feel there was no escape from him. Until today – the first time in a generation when Iraqis know beyond doubt that he will never rule them again.
>
> He was born in 1937 to a poor family … His childhood was marked from the outset by cruelty and beatings … In 1979 he immediately began the purges and killings that marked his rule. This extraordinary footage … *(SH ordering immediate execution for 'treason'; interview with former Iraqi intelligence chief about SH's psychopathic tendencies; RO voice-over continues with scenes from Halabja massacre.)*
>
> In 1988 he used chemical weapons in the attack on Halabja during the campaign against the Kurds of Northern Iraq which killed over 100,000 civilians.
>
> Saddam Hussein has not always been our enemy. Indeed, he was our ally when he committed this atrocity.
>
> And he was supported by Britain and the US in his catastrophic war against neighbouring Iran: an eight-year titanic struggle which left a million dead and wounded and in which Saddam Hussein again used chemical weapons. But for the

West he was a useful bulwark against the spread of Ayatollah Khomeni's brand of radical Islam. And so support for him was maintained.

But it was one tremendous miscalculation that put him on the path to confrontation and war with the US and Britain when Saddam Hussein sent his troops into Kuwait in 1990 ... Against all the odds he survived ... and set about re-exerting his rule with yet more purges and killings *(documentary cataloguing of officials and family members killed).*

Tonight Saddam is a prisoner – far from the palaces from which he ruled Iraq ... The Coalition easily destroyed Saddam's regime. But erasing his memory from the minds of ordinary Iraqis will take years. His capture provides that opportunity. Rageh Omaar, BBC News (14.12.03).

Rageh Omaar's review of Saddam's career mostly conforms to the news agenda firmed up during the day: the explanatory emphasis on individual biography and psychology, hubristic changes of personal fortune and the 'palaces to prison' transformation. But in the middle of the narrative comes an abrupt shift of perspective with the insertion of a political context into an otherwise pathologically-motivated life story. It may be only a brief caesura in a relentless catalogue of apparently arbitrary brutality but it is an 'however/but' type of pause that allows for the emergence of an alternative account. The qualification that 'Saddam Hussein has not always been our enemy' comes with the reminder of a different, historical account of wider global interests at stake. A small qualification and only a few lines of voice-over – but so noticeably out of sync with the rest of the news coverage that, if opened up to reflection, could undermine the dominant tale of individual hubris.

There are many ways of accounting for how any broadcast content may go against the grain – whether it's the big leaky moments or the smaller caesural modifications. Enzensberger's own analysis, for instance, highlighted inherent technological contradictions; other media researchers emphasise the conflict models involved in a political economy of broadcasting. But what I want to pick up on finally are some aspects of the 'ethos' of broadcasting, the sets of professional practices and beliefs that journalists and their news organisations, as everyday 'brokers in symbols'[5] subscribe to. I'm thinking of terms like: *public service; independence; trust; responsibility to the viewer; balance; not editorialising; impartiality* – all of which receive pretty short shrift from the accusatory perspective which either exposes them as chimerical notions ('*of course* they're not independent') or refers to them in order to catch out broadcasters who fail to live up to their promises ('that was *hardly* a balanced report').

So in conclusion, I want to suggest how taking a broadcasting ethos seriously in its own terms may contribute to understanding how professional beliefs and organisational policies get translated and negotiated into routine practices and conventions that may directly relate to leaky moments and contradictory outcomes.

To return to Rageh Omaar as a case in point. Following his stint as the BBC's chief correspondent in Iraq – he had arrived a year before the war and stayed in Baghdad for its duration – he gave a clear distillation of his broadcasting practice at a prestigious lecture to the Royal Television Society.[6] Starting with 'one amazing statistic', that more journalists were killed during the war than Coalition troops, he discusses his team's decision to remain in Baghdad on the eve of war when most of the international press corps were recalled amidst rumours that they would be used as 'human shields' by the Republican Guard. The lecture demonstrates a strong journalistic pride in having a 'responsibility' and 'duty' to witness the war from inside the Iraq capital – but witness from whose point of view? His central touchstone here is repeatedly that of 'ordinary Iraqis', particularly as, under wartime conditions, they could not tell their own story:

> *But this was the story*, and the only way of getting these views across was by editorialising, by putting the comments in my mouth … It was not reporting in the normal sense. It placed a lot of responsibility on us as journalists [because] it forced reporters to strain a key relationship based on trust – the one with the audience.

But another reason for staying in Baghdad when the BBC originally thought he should leave was that 'nearly fifty thousand of our fellow citizens had been sent to fight and possibly die in Iraq. I and my other British colleagues had a duty to inform their relatives about this war from *all* angles – and that of course included Baghdad.' It also included reporting accurately 'on the deaths of innocent Iraqis', starting with the Al Shaab massacre from an American bomb in the first week: 'The need to say and describe exactly what we saw with our own eyes was critical – and we also conveyed what eyewitnesses told us'. And, when the troops entered Baghdad, it meant pointing out that 'the threat to us was not the Republican Guard [but] from the young, American military might who'd arrived in Baghad armed to the teeth' – and on the first day had killed journalists based in the Palestine hotel.

Rageh Omaar's lecture is based on a broadcasting ethos that emphasises gaining the trust of both viewer and source and believes in a responsibility to report accurately from '*all* angles'. It must therefore take account of a range of reference groups from 'ordinary Iraqis' to the relatives of British troops. It indicates how a broadcaster deploys the notion of 'balance', not in the abstract, but as a professional practice: how it involves a constant assessment of the situation in terms of different viewpoints and a *brokerage* of those viewpoints, translating one community to another. From this perspective, it seems to me that the issue both for media studies and progressive politics is not so much whether the resulting report is correct or not but rather the recognition that 'balance' *as a practice* acknowledges concrete situations to be inherently contradictory. Thus it always offers the possibility of opening up different versions of an event – with sometimes surprising consequences.

Thus whilst political activists might think Omaar's actual reports from Baghdad didn't open up that much, this was certainly not the UK government's view. It has since emerged that the government complained to the BBC about his very presence in Baghdad, and for then daring to remain in what they now designated 'enemy territory'. The government's Director of Communications and Strategy, Alistair Campbell, has admitted only to complaining that Omaar did not make sufficiently clear the reporting restrictions he was under during his broadcasts. But there was a wider, racist, unease that as a Somali-born Muslim and fluent Arabic speaker, he was 'not one of us' in the first place. This turned to outright hostility when suggestions emanated from the Downing Street press department, in response to the remarks Omaar had made on return from Iraq about being terrified of the American troops but not of the Iraqis, that he must have 'gone native'.[7]

From this perspective, the BBC showed considerable chutzpah in nominating Omaar to give the Huw Wheldon lecture in the first place. And then following it up a month later by inviting the French Foreign Minister, Dominique de Villepin, passionately articulate and sophisticated critic of the UK invasion of Iraq, to give the Dimbleby lecture.[8] Introducing de Villepin, David Dimbleby noted how critics of the BBC spoke of the corporation as 'an arm of the government'. Clearly, he said, if that was the case we wouldn't have invited him – 'or, at least, we'd only have had him on air by interviewing him, not allowing him a platform'. He went on to point out how many people in Britain had agreed with de Villepin before the Iraq war, and even those who disagreed had paid attention to what he had to say.

This statement from a journalist who's now acquired a status similar to his father's within and outside the BBC, together with the prominence the BBC granted to both Omaar and de Villepin, indicated a bullish, up-yours attitude towards the government. It offered a symbolic assertion of independence at a moment when the BBC was experiencing itself as both severely under government attack for its coverage of the Iraq war and most publicly 'on trial' for the very credibility of its reporting.

For by then it had turned out that government hostility to Omaar's reporting merely prefigured the all-out opposition to come. Government criticism of Omaar remained mainly covert at the time, probably because his reports were actually often quite cautious, rather bland, interpretations of 'balance', and also because of his high ratings and audience popularity.[9] Whereas the BBC reporter Andrew Gilligan who became the *casus belli* for overt government criticism of the BBC was a spikier, more obviously pushy journalist, with a reputation for gaining 'exclusive' stories in the field of defence.

As with Omaar, the government had started out covertly critical of Gilligan's war reports, which also came from Baghdad and were transmitted on BBC Radio 4's *Today* current affairs magazine. But the criticism became overt following the now famous item on the *Today* programme, the first story in the three-hour slot. The item referred to the dossier the government had published in September 2002 setting out its concerns about the threat posed by Iraq. Andrew Gilligan went on to explain:

> I have spoken to a British official who was involved in the preparation of the dossier
> and he told me that until a week before it was published, the draft dossier produced by
> the intelligence services added little to what was already publicly known. He said:
> *(actor's voiceover)* 'It was transformed in the week before it was published to make it
> sexier. The classic example was the statement that weapons of mass destruction were
> ready for use within 45 minutes. That information was not in the original draft … Most
> things in the dossier were double source, but that was single source and we believed
> the source was wrong'.
>
> Now this official told us that the transformation … took place at the behest of Downing
> Street and he added: *(voice-over)* 'Most people in intelligence weren't happy with the
> dossier because it didn't reflect the considered view that they were putting forward.'
>
> … Now the forty-five minutes really is not just a detail, it did go to the heart of the
> case that Saddam was an imminent threat, and it was repeated a further three times
> in the dossier … (BBC R4, 6.07am, 29.05.05).

The government via Alistair Campbell demanded an immediate retraction of this story (which Gilligan had amplified the following weekend in his *Mail on Sunday* column, specifically naming Campbell as responsible for the 'sexing up'). But after a series of private communications with the BBC had failed to elicit an apology, the row become public when Campbell issued an open letter to the BBC (26.06.03) demanding that twelve points challenging the story be responded to that day. The BBC immediately replied through its Director of News, Richard Sambrook:

> We stand by our entire story. In my experience, this is an unprecedented level of
> pressure on the BBC from Downing Street. The BBC will respond properly to these
> matters, but not to a deadline dictated by Mr Campbell.

The following day, the BBC issued a public rebuttal of all twelve points, refusing to apologise or to reveal its source. During this May-June period, the Foreign Affairs Committee (FAC), one of the select parliamentary bodies that scrutinises government departments, had been conducting an enquiry on 'The Decision to Go to War in Iraq'. When it published its findings at the beginning of July, it criticised the government's lack of 'co-operation' with parliament over intelligence evidence, maintained an open mind on the evidence for weapons of mass destruction and challenged the second, February 2003, dossier, which the press had already exposed as 'dodgy' for its inaccuracies and plagiarism, and for which Campbell was primarily responsible. But it entirely exonerated Campbell over the 'sexing up' allegation (08.07.03).

This was not sufficient for Campbell, who was later to reveal from his diaries of the time that he wanted a clear 'win' over the BBC, not a 'draw'. The following day, via the Ministry of Defence, he effected the 'outing' of Gilligan's source, with the aim of discrediting him, and hence Gilligan and the BBC, on the grounds that the source was not actually involved in intelligence and hence not in a position to convey reliable evidence. Dr David Kelly, chief scientific officer and senior adviser to the Ministry of Defence on weapons proliferation and arms control, was duly called to give evidence to FAC, where he challenged the 45-minute claim but denied he was Gilligan's source (15.07.03). Two days later, he committed suicide. A shaken Tony Blair, in Japan after delivering a triumphant speech to the US Congress on the theme 'history will forgive us' for the war in Iraq, announced that a judicial enquiry into all the circumstances surrounding Dr Kelly's death would be chaired by respected law lord Lord Hutton. The BBC immediately acknowledged that Kelly had indeed been the source of the *Today* story.

Throughout August and September the Hutton Enquiry took evidence – in public session and with daily internet records – from civil servants, intelligence officers, government scientists, ministers, the prime minister, Kelly's family, BBC reporters, managers and chairman, as well as from Gilligan and Campbell. At the end of August, Campbell resigned from government service and returned to freelance journalism.

In the hiatus before Hutton reported and as the post-war occupation of Iraq proved increasingly unstable and dangerous, doubts about the existence of WMD and the original justifications for war started to be publicly expressed by former officials and advisers of both British and American administrations. In this climate, where polling in both countries demonstrated an increasing public scepticism about the war and occupation, Lord Hutton's findings were completely unexpected when his report was published at the end of January 2004. Apart from a minor criticism of the Ministry of Defence for the way Dr Kelly had been outed, the government, and Campbell as its chief spokesman, were completely exonerated of all blame in the entire affair, whilst the BBC was castigated from top to bottom for making 'very grave' and unfounded claims against the government. The Chairman of the BBC Governors immediately resigned; the BBC Director-General, then failing to secure the backing of a panicked Governing Body, also resigned; the Acting Chair of Governors issued an unreserved apology to the government; the Acting Director-General announced a further far-reaching enquiry into the conduct of news and current affairs and Andrew Gilligan resigned.

From this bald outline of events it would be easy to sum up with a picture of a cowed and demoralised broadcasting institution forced to submit to the government's agenda. But I think the story points just as much to a 'paradox of the consequences' and a series of unplanned and unpredictable outcomes. Thus, whilst the BBC immediately went into extreme abject mode in its official responses to the Hutton enquiry, nobody else did. BBC personnel in London and at all regional centres protested against the apologies being made in their name and declared their loyalty to the departing Director-General. Meanwhile, the British press came out, uniquely and unanimously, in support of the BBC, declaring the Hutton Report a complete 'whitewash' of the government and a threat to both press and broadcasting freedoms, with its narrowly legalistic interpretation of the role of journalistic sources and evidence. Furthermore, the very stark pro-government/anti-BBC conclusions of the Report were widely perceived to be dramatically out of kilter with the whole tenor of the evidence gathered in the summer. Indeed, the very transparency of the Hutton proceedings, with its diary and e-mail revelations, had afforded an unsettling glimpse into the workings of a government obsessively anxious about a programme 'nobody' had listened to in the first place – the summoning of so many emergency top-level meetings, swirling rumours, macho bullying, dubious equivocations. However little attention anyone might have paid to the nitty-gritty detail of the Enquiry, you could hardly escape the impression of dodgy conduct on the government's behalf. Thus opinion-polling in the week following the publication of the Hutton Report showed just how counter-productive its conclusions had been for the government. There were solid expressions of public confidence in the BBC, support for its editorial policies and continued independence from government, and a corresponding disbelief in the government's dossier claims, with such a loss of public trust that, for instance, 51 per cent of respondents in one poll declared Blair should resign immediately (NOP poll, *Independent on Sunday*, 07.02.04).

There are many contradictory factors to take into account in any consideration of how it happened that one small item on a radio programme should have become so hugely symbolic of the relation between government and media. But in returning to the issue of taking broadcasting ethos and policy seriously, I want to conclude by referring to just two aspects: the editorial practices of balance and impartiality and the institutional defence of broadcasting's independence from government.

When Alistair Campbell went before the FAC enquiry in June 2003, he used the example of the *Today* programme to demonstrate that, all along, the BBC had had an anti-war, anti-government agenda. Hence his obsession with a 'win' over the BBC and the need, as expressed in his diary entries submitted to Hutton, to *'fuck* Gilligan' and thereby the BBC. Any empirical examination of the BBC's Iraq coverage would easily demonstrate that Campbell's claims were ludicrous – and indeed, many commentators, as I've noted, have suggested that the BBC actually remained far too close to a government agenda during the war.

But there is also a sense in which Campbell perceived something that might actually be quite heartening for those who did indeed oppose the war. Namely that, because the policies of balance and impartiality have written into them a requirement for journalists to assume that a government's statements can never stand as *the* only, unchallenged, perspective on a situation, they inevitably encourage the search for other perspectives. And however tentatively and 'unequally' those other views are then communicated, in certain situations their very expression may be pivotal. Thus the very extremity of Campbell's and the government's reaction to one tiny 'leak' in a radio programme served to indicate the increasing shakiness of the government's justification for war in Iraq.

At the same time, the fallout from Hutton may have actually left the BBC in a more powerful position in relation to the government. For the widespread public demonstration of support for the corporation pushed the government to insist on its own respect for the BBC's autonomy and to promise no interference in the choice of the new Chair of the Governors. When Michael Grade was appointed to that post he immediately reaffirmed his belief in the BBC's editorial impartiality, declaring that there would be no more apologies and that he would serve as a faithful guarantor of the BBC's independence. His fighting talk on this occasion recalled the spirit the BBC had shown at the start of the *Today* affair when the management had first defended the Gilligan story.

When Richard Sambrook rebutted Campbell's criticism of the story point by point, his open letter began with a wider statement:

> Dear Alistair, … Before I answer the questions in detail I wish to explain the wider context in which we came to broadcast the story.
>
> 1. Allegations of biased reporting: … It is our firm view that No 10 tried to intimidate the BBC in its reporting of events leading up to the war and during the course of the war itself.
>
> As we told you in correspondence before the war started, our responsibility was to present an impartial picture and you were not best placed to judge what was impartial. This was particularly the case given the widescale opposition to the war in the UK at the time, including significant opposition inside the parliamentary Labour party (28.06.03).

This letter indicates how, in assessing its journalistic coverage, the BBC is constantly engaged in scrutinising 'the balance of forces' on the ground. And the initial robustness of the BBC's response to government pressure in 2003, I suggest, cannot be divorced from the huge explosion of protest in the lead-up to the war, particularly the demonstration of 15 February in the capital (with claims varying from 1- 2 million participants, but universally agreed to be the largest-ever in the UK). The demonstration made visible a large constituency of dissent within the country and in parliament itself, that simply could not be ignored by any broadcasting organisation maintaining a stance of independence from government. Both the visible diversity and size of the demonstration gave a legitimacy to dissent which, even though it could not stop the war, allowed for some widening of the scope, *at the very least,* of what constituted broadcasting's definitions of 'balance' and 'impartiality' and enabled it to resist a government-imposed agenda.

Notes

1. David Miller (Ed.), *Tell Me Lies*, Pluto Press, London, 2003.
2. See H.M.Enzensberger, 'Constituents of a Theory of the Media', first published in English in *New Left Review*, Vol. 64, November-December 1970, and in abbreviated form in D. McQuail (Ed.), *Sociology of Mass Communications*, Penguin Books, Harmondsworth, 1972. This influential article was originally conceived as a polemic against the post-'68 Left's undue fear of media 'manipulation' and their refusal to engage with the democratic potential of the new information technologies.
3. The Dixie Chicks, a US girl band, had recently criticised the impending war and a number of their gigs had been cancelled amidst widespread public condemnation. Moore's Oscar-winning speech was widely reprised on British television, especially at end of year reviews; e.g. it came 30th in *The 100 Greatest TV Treats of 2003*, admiringly introduced by BBC Iraq reporter Rageh Omaar.
4. From *Letters the Troops Have Sent Me*, Michael Moore, 19.12.03, and widely circulated via Stop the War Coalition mail-lists in the UK.
5. This term was coined by James W. Carey in his seminal article, 'The Communication Revolution and the Professional Communicator', first published in Paul Halmos (Ed.), *The Sociology of Mass Communicators, Sociological Review Monograph, no 13*, Keele University, Jan. 1969.
6. This was the annual BBC lecture in honour of Huw Wheldon, a celebrated administrator, presenter and producer of innovative BBC-TV arts programmes in the 1960s. It was delivered in Cambridge, 18.09.03, and subsequently broadcast in its entirety on BBC-2, 22.09.03. All quotations from Rageh Omaar here come from this lecture.
7. Information from contemporary press sources and most explicitly outlined in Simon Hattenstone's profile, 'Reluctant Warrior', *Guardian Weekend* magazine, 28.02.04, marking the publication of Rageh Omaar's book about his war experiences, *Revolution Day*, Viking, March 2004.
8. This, the 'other' prestigious annual lecture in the BBC TV calendar, is in honour of Richard Dimbleby, one of the first presenters of *Panorama*, the longest-lasting BBC TV current affairs programme, and a commentator at key state occasions like the Coronation and funeral of Winston Churchill. The lecture, broadcast on BBC 1, 19.10.03, called on Britain and France to come together in shaping Europe's future and included criticism of the USA's 'unilateralist' use of force and comments on how occupiers of countries continued to believe, against all historical evidence, that the occupied were never capable of ruling themselves.
9. For instance, Omaar received the tabloid soubriquet 'Scud Stud' for his good looks; was voted *Radio Times* Man of the Year in 2003 and placed on *RT's* 'Television's Most Wanted Men' list in 2004.

Guidelines for Contributors

Each issue is planned around a theme. Prospective writers are encouraged to contact the editor to discuss their ideas. Please keep in mind that we aim for an accessible style of writing, free of jargon and aimed at communicating with a general non-fiction audience as well as academic and student markets. The titles of articles and general phrasing should avoid academic orthodoxy.

Keep references to a minimum. Notes should be used for referencing sources, rather than indicating other books or essays in the same field. They should be numbered in the Chicago style, using superscript. All notes should be placed at the end of the article.

No Bibliographies.

Essays should be between 5,000 and 6,000 words long. Please post one copy to

Jonathan Rutherford, Editor
Mediactive
Media Communications and Cultural Studies
Middlesex University
White Hart Lane
London N17 8HR

Send an email attachment in Word to J.rutherford@mdx.ac.uk or to the issue editor. Please include:

1. A 100-word synopsis to introduce the article. This will appear on the first page of the article, after the title;
2. A couple of sentences to describe yourself, for inclusion on the notes on contributors page.

Copyright
Submissions of a paper to *Mediactive* will be taken to imply that it presents original, unpublished work not under consideration for publication elsewhere. By submitting a manuscript the author agrees that he or she is granting the Publisher for a fixed term the exclusive right to reproduce and distribute the paper including reprints, photographic reproductions, microfilm or any other reproduction of a similar nature, and translations. He or she will not be required to assign the copyright.

Notes
Use a superscript number in the text. Each reference should follow this basic format: name, *book*, publisher date.

Note the commas. Book in italics, no brackets around publisher. p6, not p.6 or p. 6; pp67-69 not pp. 67-69 or pp.67-69; op cit not op. cit.; ibid not ibid.

A more detailed version of this guide is available from the editor and will be sent out to contributors. Please check your copy against the guide before sending it to the editor.

Notes on Contributors

Darren J. O'Byrne is Senior Lecturer in Sociology and Human Rights at the University of Roehampton. He is the author of *Human Rights: An Introduction* (Longman, 2002) and *The Dimensions of Global Citizenship* (Frank Cass, 2003), and is currently working on an edited volume on global ethics and civil society. He is also the Chair of the Global Studies Association.

Rosalind Brunt is Research Fellow in Media Studies at Sheffield Hallam University. She has written widely in the areas of media studies and popular culture and is currently working on an EU action research project examining media representations of Arabs and Muslims.

Cynthia Carter is Lecturer in the Cardiff School of Journalism, Media and Cultural Studies, Cardiff University. Her research interests include: children, news and citizenship; gender, journalism and news; media violence; and news reports of health risks. She is co-author of *Violence and the Media* (2003) and co-editor of *Critical Readings: Media and Gender* (2004), *Environmental Risks and the Media* (2000) and *News, Gender and Power* (1998). She also co-edits the academic journal *Feminist Media Studies*.

Des Freedman is a lecturer in communications and cultural studies in the Department of Media and Communications at Goldsmiths College. He is the author of *The Television Policies of the Labour Party* (Frank Cass 2003) and co-editor of a recent collection of essays on the relationship between journalists and conflict, *War and the Media* (Sage 2003).

Ramaswami Harindranath is Senior Lecturer in Media and Communications at the University of Melbourne, Australia. He co-edited *Approaches to Audiences*, and co-authored *The Crash Controversy: Censorship Campaigns and Film Reception*. He is currently completing a manuscript on cultural imperialism to be published by Pluto Press in 2005.

Patricia Holland is the author of *The Television Handbook* (Routledge, 2000, 2nd edition) and *Picturing Childhood: the myth of the child in popular imagery* (I. B. Tauris, 2003) as well as numerous articles on aspects of the media. She is researching the history of current affairs television.

Jake Lynch is an experienced international reporter in television and print media, and Co-Director of the journalism think-tank, Reporting the World.

Máire Messenger Davies is Professor at the University of Ulster, Coleraine. A psychologist and former journalist, she is the author of a number of books and reports on children and the media, including *'Dear BBC': Children, Television, Storytelling and the Public Sphere* (CUP, 2001) and, with Nick Mosdell, *Consenting Children? The Use of Children in Non-Fiction Television Programmes* (Broadcasting Standards Commission, 2001).

Paul Rixon is a Senior Lecturer at the University of Surrey Roehampton. His research interests include American television, new media creativity and media technologies.

Daya Thussu teaches transnational communications and global media at Goldsmiths College, University of London. Among his publications are *Contra-Flow in Global News* (John Libbey in association with UNESCO, 1992); *Electronic Empires – Global Media and Local Resistance* (Arnold, 1998); *International Communication – Continuity and Change* (Arnold, 2000) and *War and the Media – Reporting Conflict 24/7* (Sage, 2003).

Past and future issues

Mediactive bridges the gap between universities and public debate, engaging with contemporary issues of politics and culture; it uses theoretical concepts, but tries to be free of jargon – aiming at a general non-fiction readership as well as an academic market. The principle idea is the fast and effective publication of good quality writing and scholarly work, and the use of modern technologies to reduce costs to a minimum.

Issue 1 Knowledge/Culture (2003)

Mediactive 1 looks at the revolutionary changes being made in the provision of public forms of education in the UK, largely instituted by policies informed by neoliberalism. The changes to practices of knowledge creation and academic life are paradigmatic, and we need to understand these new conditions, and to create a language and politics which can reassert the value of knowledge and education as public goods. The issue includes: an analysis of the nature of knowledge; discussion on New Labour and the knowledge economy, cultural studies as an area of contestation, the commodification of education and news journalism; new thoughts on science and culture; and a rethinking of intellectual work in the digital age. **Contributors** Clare Birchall, Lynda Dyson, Alan Finlayson, Andrew Goffey, Gary Hall, Glenn Rikowski, Jonathan Rutherford.

Issue 2 Celebrity, edited by Jo Littler (2004)

Mediactive 2 investigates the world of celebrity. From the talented to the simply over exposed, celebrities feed the media machine with a display of wealth, scandal and glamour, fuelling our fascination with the imitate details of other people's lives, loves and foibles. The issue includes a discussion on reality tv; an analysis of the Blair family's celebrity status; a debate about intimacy and 'keeping it real'; a look at cult tv fan cultures; and a discussion about popstars trying (and usually failing) to be actors. Contributors Anita Biressi, Kay Dickinson, Jeremy Gilbert, Matt Hills, Jo Littler, Heather Nunn, Oscar Reyes.

Issue 4 Asylum (2005)

Issue 4 takes on asylum. What does the widespread circulation of hateful and racist representations of migrants, and the individual paranoia invoked by cultural difference, tell us about European cultures? Can we create a collective response to migration that is based on mutual give and take, and an ethic of concern for the other? The issue includes: the meaning of being a good neighbour; the dynamics of hate and xenophobia; the cashing-in of corporations; the politics of human security; refugees/asylum seekers as the coming *condition humaine*; ideas for a new European identity. **Contributors** Zygmunt Bauman, Rosemary Bechler, Farhad Dalal, Richard Payne, Jonathan Rutherford, Nira Yuval-Davis.

For further details and to buy copies: www.barefootpublications.co.uk

Mediactive gratefully acknowledges the financial support of the Barry Amiel and Norman Melburn Trust and the School of Arts, Middlesex University.